F'd UP

The UPside of Failure

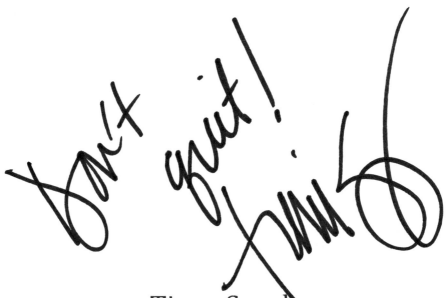

Tiana Sanchez

Tian M. Daniels

First Printing, 2016

Printed in the United States of America

Efluential Publishing

Table of Contents

Dedication

I thank God for blessing me with the ability to inspire others through writing and speaking. I dedicate this book to my grandmother Dorma, the first woman entrepreneur I ever met. You taught me the meaning of work ethic and perseverance. For that I am eternally grateful.

Author Manifesto

I believe there is no limit to your success! I work in tandem with colleges and employers to foster a more confident and competent workforce. Through leader-led workshops and competency-based learning, I help people develop the skills they need to perform better in their careers. My passion for helping others raise the bar and remove limitations was spawned through years in management and honed during an impressive and longstanding career in the retail, food and beverage, and financial industries. At age seventeen, I was one of the youngest managers overseeing day-to-day business operations and directing employee development. A pivotal moment in my career was when I was appointed by the CEO of a financial institution to join a strategic planning team, sparking my interest in organizational development and establishing me as a skilled speaker.

My greatest achievement was nurturing employees' potential and moving them up the career ladder. In 2011, I launched Tiana Sanchez Professional Coaching Services, an organizational training and development practice. Focused on leaders, managers, emerging leaders, young adults, and students, individuals RE-THINK their leadership potential and RE-DEFINE success. Redefining success means embracing one's failures. But this passion is not without controversy.

Some people with antiquated views and closed minds are reluctant to use failures as learning opportunities, putting in place harsh consequences for learners. I've seen good, hard-working employees "managed out" or let go due to poor performance without an opportunity to improve. I've seen students become discouraged when they fail because they are not encouraged that there is an upside to failure. When did we stop helping people become better? We have become a culture that praises intelligence over effort. Systems are established and designed to reward the high achievers and weed out the so-called low achievers—leaving the low-achievers up the creek without a paddle. I propose a different solution: develop a culture where failure is viewed as information one can use to solve problems and enhance overall learning and skill development.

Failure is information we can use to solve a problem. It's where *I can't* and *I will* intersect. It's where you overcome the doubt that comes with failure and embrace the motivation you need to push through. There *is* an upside to unintentional failure.

This book will provide insight into why some people view failures as opportunities and a necessary step toward success while others simply quit or have an aversion to the effort required to push through. In my first book, *Undefeatable*, the message is clear: failure is inevitable. The upside to failure is that although it is inevitable (it *will* happen), failure is also an opportunity to learn. Failures teach us critical thinking, creative problem-solving skills, effort (work required), and attitude (motivation). We are a culture that does not always embrace work. We would rather quit instead of encouraging our own learning and gaining new and better information. We often get offended if we are not seen as competent or highly talented. When an unintentional failure does occur, most of us revert to a defeated mindset and accept the outcome.

This book is not just theory; it is based on my real-life experience. Professionally, I have over twenty years of experience leading and managing both high-performing and under-performing teams. Personally, I have been unemployed, broke, and homeless. This rare perspective qualifies me to speak candidly on the topic of failure, and my unique experience gives me a decidedly different vantage point than most. My hope is to clarify and debunk the misconceptions we have about failure through the words in this book.

Many of us believe that failures are inherently bad and fatal to our career, life, and relationships. In my opinion, however, failure opens up a new pathway of unexplored strength and resolve. That strength and resolve would never have otherwise been realized had we not experienced the failure in the first place. This book introduces a paradigm shift regarding how we view failure as a culture. So, readers, I'm asking you to have an open mind. Be willing to embrace new ideas and new concepts. Challenge yourself to think differently and beyond the box. Some of you may need to throw out the box entirely to grasp this idea.

This book is for Success-Creators, not Doubt-Creators. It's for educators who have an open mind and embrace new methods rather than settling for teaching outdated ones. This book is for organizations who believe that there are other ways to correct behavior and performance that do not rely solely on penalties and punishment. And to my young adults and emerging leaders, this book is for you. There is no limit to your success! Period.

Chapter 1

The UPside of Failure

"Success is not final, failure is not fatal: it is the courage to continue that counts."
—Winston Churchill

Look upon failure as a friend and not the enemy—not likely your best friend or your BFF, but a friend that tells you the hard truth. Failure is a friend that tells you what you *need* to hear, not just what you want to hear. It's the kind of friend that pushes you out of your comfort zone and shows you a new way to look at things. When I wrote my first book, I had no idea how it would be received by others. The book launched in the summer of 2013 at an intimate book-signing event in Beverly Hills, California. Fifty of my closest family and friends joined me to celebrate the release of this book and hear the story behind it: losing my job, starting a business ninety days later, and writing my first book. Wow!

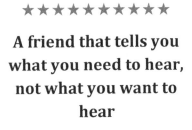

A friend that tells you what you need to hear, not what you want to hear

The feedback was good, but of course they were my friends and I had to go outside of my circle to gain some objective feedback. I was invited to speak at conferences and local events to inspire and motivate others through what I had experienced—my story. I began speaking at colleges and universities to undergraduate students and faculty. And a miraculous thing occurred. One of the administrators at a university asked to purchase one hundred copies of the book to give away as reading material for her students. She deemed the message in the book—failure is inevitable, but defeat is optional—as highly valuable and critical for students, especially students with little real-world experience. This

The kind of friend that pushes you out of your comfort zone and shows you a new way to look at things

was a pivotal moment in my writing career, and it was at that very moment that I realized something revolutionary and significant. There was an audience of young adults and emerging leaders out there that needed to hear this message on failure. Out of that experience and realization, this book was birthed. The door swung wide open, and I gratefully entered, sharing this message with hundreds of people—which, poignantly, turned out to be the "upside" to many of my failures.

Over the past two years, I've spoken to hundreds of high school students, college-bound students, and undergraduate students of all ages, colors, and ethnicities. The response has been remarkable. While speaking at one particular leadership conference, a four-year management student approached me after my talk and shared how valuable this information was to him. He hopped up on stage with me and he, along with other students in the audience, took what we later coined a #conferenceselfie. This young man took the time to send me a follow-up email, and here's what he wrote:

I wanted to write and thank you for your presentation in the fall semester at the University of California, Merced, September 26, 2015.

Your talk was AWESOME! I wish more students across the world could hear your message! Your message has impacted me to be more confident through life and school.

Once again, thank you. We, the students, wish you could come back!

Best Regards,

Phila Justice Gcaba
Fourth Year Management Student
University of California, Merced

As a writer and speaker, this type of feedback inspires me. It's the satisfaction of knowing that he got it! He understood and was changed. It's when I tell myself, "Mission accomplished." But in reality, my mission was only beginning.

My first book, *Undefeatable*, was written for anyone who had experienced failures. If you had experienced failure, this book was for you. If you had ever given up or quit anything, this book was for you. If you ever looked at failure as something to frown upon, this book was for you. If you had ever been defeated by your failures, this book was for you. Conquering self-defeat is the internal battle of

Conquering self-defeat is the internal battle of wanting to quit and the need to push through.

wanting to quit and the need to push through. It is the emotional battle of getting back up after getting knocked down. How do you stay out of the defeated zone of self-pity, depression, and self-loathing? The message sharpened our lenses of how we view losses, failures, and wins.

The upside of (unintentional) failure is the aftermath, the time of reflection, and the birth of new ideas. It's what we can learn about ourselves and the specific skills that we can gain from that failure or unsuccessful experience—skills like critical thinking and creative problem-solving. The upside is the *benefit of opening up a new pathway of unexplored strength and resolve, which would have not otherwise been realized had we not experienced the failure in the first place.*

As children, we are taught to win, win, and win! You have to be the best, and in order to be the best you need to win. Losing is unacceptable. We don't tolerate failures. Imagine hearing those words growing up. Now that wasn't my story, but I imagine there are many of you reading this that can relate. The message in my home was not to win but simply to stay above water to keep from drowning, figuratively speaking.

Seventeen Reasons Not to Quit

If I were to ask you to recall the number of times you moved or changed residences over the course of your life, could you remember? I can—seventeen. That is the number of times I've moved since I've been on this earth. I've lived in apartments, a house with relatives, a woman's shelter for abused women (I was a child at the time), a shabby motel, and for one night, I slept in my car. I remember curling up with a blanket in the back seat and wondering how I got there. Our experiences do not define us, but how we push through the adversity is what defines us. I am grateful

★ ★ ★ ★ ★ ★ ★ ★ ★ ★

Our experiences do not define us, but how we push through the adversity is what defines us.

★ ★ ★ ★ ★ ★ ★ ★ ★ ★

for my experiences. They have given me wisdom, perspective, and appreciation. In addition, my experiences have helped countless others push through their "stuff."

I was seventeen when I started working full time as a manager at a gourmet fast-food restaurant at the local mall in my hometown of Hawthorne, California. I was still in high school, a senior in fact, with less than a year left to graduation. Working was not a luxury; it was a necessity. A student's last year in high school is probably the most expensive year any student or parent will experience. A rundown of costs may look like this: prom, yearbook, class ring, senior pictures, graduation, grad night, and a car (optional). Now imagine being seventeen years old and having to pay for all of this. Being self-sufficient taught me how to be responsible as well as the value of hard work. I developed a strong work ethic and learned to be frugal, saving more than I spent. That type of life experience is invaluable, and the work experience I gained was priceless.

Before starting my own business in 2011, I spent seventeen years working in the food and beverage, clothing, furniture, and financial industries. I led teams and managed day-to-day operations. Throughout my career, I was responsible for training and developing staff, recruiting new talent, and hiring and onboarding new managers. Managing the day-to-day operations lacked the excitement of managing people, but I learned about financial reports and budgets. I excelled in my role and sat on the strategic planning team for one organization, tasked with helping to set the direction for the company's future. I worked directly with the CEO and key executives, whose pay grades were well above mine. I was in the company of individuals who made millions, collectively. One would say, and I would agree, that I had a relatively successful career if one defined success by way of promotion, good pay, recognition, and awards. It was certainly not a bad career for someone without a degree who worked her way up the career ladder to make a good living and enjoy meaningful work. However, after seventeen years, the career that I knew was over. The loss of my job was an unexpected "failure" that propelled me forward like a cannon ball out of a cannon. I often wonder if I would be where I am now if I had not experienced losing my job. I'm reminded of my earlier statement:

Failure opens up a new pathway of unexplored strength and resolve, which would not have otherwise been realize had we not experienced the failure in the first place.

Failure, in my opinion, opens up a new pathway of unexplored strength and resolve, which would not have otherwise been realized had we not experienced the failure in the first place.

Each experience taught me something new. Moving around more than seventeen times taught me to value consistency and appreciate stability in my life. Taking on the responsibility and working full time while in school, and managing before the age of eighteen, taught me to not doubt myself and my God-given talents. Letting go of a career to pursue living a meaningful and fulfilling life—doing work that I loved—was one of the biggest lessons learned. Quitting was not an option for me, nor does it have to be an option for you. It is my privilege to impress upon you some of the lessons I've learned, primarily the upside of failure.

Failure is not something we talk openly about. We protect our self-image by pretending it doesn't apply to us. We see failure as weak and as a deficiency. If we are honest with ourselves, we would rather lie about our failures than

We choose to blindfold the truth instead of choosing transparency.

utter the words "I've failed" to someone. We choose to blindfold the truth instead of choosing transparency. My mission is to change that, but how do we change something that's been embedded into our culture for years?

I'm Not Giving Up

Did you learn how to deal with your failures when you were a kid? If you know how to walk, ride a bike, skate, or swim, then your answer is probably a yes. The message was simple: "If you fall, you get right back up." We didn't worry about falling because we knew we would. It was a certainty, a definite in a world of possibilities. We fell with grace, our confidence shaken but not defeated. Somehow, as we got older, the message became tainted and we started to see the fall as a death sentence. Why does this happen? Are we not as resilient as we once were as children?

Kids are resilient and tough. As a child, all your parents wanted to do was protect you. From the day you were born until the end of their days, they will always want to protect you. Parents (including myself) will read every book imaginable on safety and childproofing the house so that not even Houdini himself could get into that locked cabinet. They shield you from germs, bugs, and electrical things. They strap you in car seats, booster seats, and make sure you wear your seatbelt when you are old enough to drive. Parents are predictors of bad things. They will think of every possible bad scenario imaginable and then find a way to protect you from it. But can they protect you from everything? Have you ever slipped and fallen? Broken a bone? Gotten into an accident? Fallen off of a bike? Did you ever run into a wall after being chased by your older sister? Okay, I know that last one was a little specific, so let me come clean.

At about ten years old, I was chasing my brother down a hallway during an innocent game of tag. It was a very long hallway, and we were playing; we were kids—that's what we did. All laughs and giggles soon turned to cries of pain after my brother ran face first into a wall. He was so busy running away from me, and looking over his shoulder to see how close I was getting, that he didn't see the big wall that was in front of him. Blood, sweat, tears, and a call to the paramedics made the experience quite frightening. He survived; he was all right. Would injury hinder him from ever running again? Would he not play with me anymore for fear of an accident? Nope. Children are resilient.

We didn't worry about falling because we knew we would. It was a certainty, a definite in a world of possibilities. We fell with grace, our confidence shaken but not defeated.

It's virtually impossible to protect your children from everything, so the responsible thing to do is to teach them how to deal with the aftermath of accidents or mistakes. What do you do when things don't go as planned? I have two sons, and my younger son struggled badly with losing. If he didn't win at any game, he would get upset and stomp out of the room. I first noticed this phenomenon when we played a game of Uno when he was about four years old. He took to the game quickly and played remarkably well. We played the first game, and he won. We played the second game, and he won. We played the third game, and he lost. That loss caused a tsunami of tears and tantrums. Why was he reacting so badly after he won the first two times? It didn't dawn me until later that he had been playing Uno with his grandmother who always let him win. That was the first big mistake. She was a mother and wanted to protect him from experiencing a loss. I was a mother who wanted to teach him how to overcome one. He got accustomed to winning and the excitement that comes with it. So, when he actually experienced a loss, he didn't know quite how to handle it. It was time for a teaching moment.

To avoid a recurrence, I had to act fast. I pulled him aside and sat him down on the sofa next to me. I wanted to reassure him that I wasn't angry, so I sat him close to me, talking *to* him and not *at* him. I asked him why he was upset and why he quit playing the game. Children at that age are very innocent and honest, so there was no shortage of reasons why he was upset. As he talked and I listened, this helped to calm him down. I was breaking the wall down piece by piece, so that I could offer some words of wisdom. When we

When we are in our feelings and in our emotions we don't listen and are not receptive to feedback.

are in our feelings and in our emotions, we don't listen and are not receptive to feedback. However, when we experience a temporary setback, we **need to** reflect and ask ourselves some questions. I explained to him that I had been playing Uno a lot longer and had more experience with the game. I explained to him that losing simply meant that the game was over and that we could play again. And in doing so, he would learn how to play better. To seal the deal, I explained that giving up and running away from the table meant that mommy would not play with him anymore. I can't be 100 percent certain, but I think that last one did the trick. It's incredible what a difference two years can make. Now when I observe him playing a game or having difficulty getting something done, I hear him say, "I'm not giving up."

A New Society Reimagined

Imagine a society where failure is viewed as information to solve problems and to enhance learning and development. The idea would be introduced in childhood and reinforced in school and the workplace. Employers would use failures as learning opportunities to coach and mentor employees. These employees would be given opportunity to correct mistakes in an environment that supported an occasional misstep or stumble. Employers would recognize that effort in pushing through adversity

Employers would recognize that effort in pushing through adversity is a skill worth developing, not criticizing.

is a skill worth developing not criticizing. Employers would hire individuals with creative problem-solving skills and critical thinking skills. Employers would ask thought-provoking questions in interviews that explore situations where potential employees failed and how they handled that situation. Employers would see less turnover as more employees are retained and managers become more invested in their employees' development. Managers would see the employees' potential and not their shortcomings. It would be an environment of possibilities, not limitations. Failures would become part of personal development conversations that would help identify employee learning gaps.

In school and at higher education institutions, teachers, professors, and general faculty would have open minds about new teaching methods. Educators would align classroom curriculum with real-world experiences. Educators would learn the value of praising effort, not just intelligence. Students would see their failed attempts as temporary setbacks and be encouraged to find new ways to accomplish their goals.

Students would see their failed attempts as temporary setbacks and be encouraged to find new ways to accomplish their goal.

The upside of failure is wisdom. Who will benefit from what you have learned? How will it help you and others lead a better and more fulfilling life? Who and what will you impact because you decided not to give up?

Now Do This!

Scan the box below or type the URL into your browser and watch a video of Tiana speaking about her *Undefeatable* book. Select the video

"Phenomenal Women with Tiana Sanchez"

http://nolimit2yoursuccess.com/talks/

Chapter 2

Failure Is the New Success

"If you don't try at anything, you can't fail ... it takes
back bone to lead the life you want" —
Richard Yates

One day in August, I was preparing a presentation for a speaking engagement at a university the following month. The topic was *Failure Is the New Success*. In my talks, I like to share stories and examples of real-life people, and I often turn to YouTube for inspirational videos. I stumbled across this one video of female athlete Heather Dorniden running the 600-meter race at the 2008 Big Ten Indoor Track Championships. The quality of the video wasn't that great, but it was a short video so I decided to watch it. Heather and her three other competitors were in position, ready to take off.

The answer lies in how you process your failures and how your thoughts differ from others when they encounter failures.

The gun goes off and they start running. Fifty-five seconds into the race, Heather takes the lead. She looks strong, fierce, and capable of winning, yet within a matter of seconds that all changes. Heather falls flat on her face at fifty-eight seconds into the race. A misstep, a public tumble, and one embarrassing fall. What do you do when you fall flat on your face? If you are Heather Dorniden, you get up and continue running. She's far behind her competitors, and this is the last leg of the race. She's running and she's running and she's running. You can hear the audience cheering her on as she accelerates, her long legs moving in perfect stride. She is a trained athlete willing herself to the finish line. She's unstoppable, unmoved, and unshaken by her recent stumble. She's focused and capable. Heather finished strong and won the race. What a feat! How far will you go and how hard will you push to win your race?

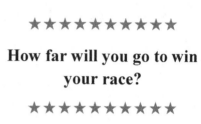

★ ★ ★ ★ ★ ★ ★ ★ ★ ★

How far will you go to win your race?

★ ★ ★ ★ ★ ★ ★ ★ ★ ★

What is success? Define it. In the space below, and in your own words, I want you to write a single sentence definition for the word success. Let this story inspire your definition.

_____

_____

Now look at your definition. Is this the world's definition of success? I challenge you to make it more personal and consider not using words like wealth, money, status, or position. Why do we care so much about success? Why do some people succeed while others do not? Have you ever considered what goes through your mind when you fail? The answer lies in how you process your failures and how your thoughts differ from others when they encounter failures.

Carol Dweck, famous psychologist and author of *Mindset: The New Psychology of Success*, understands better than most people do why some people give up in the face of failure while others are motivated to learn from their mistakes and improve. Dweck has spent her career studying these behaviors in children and adults and has concluded that fixed mindsets versus growth mindsets play an integral role in understanding this concept. In a March 2007 Stanford alumni article titled "The Effort Effect," the author wrote:

> *Dweck speculated that the difference between the helpless response and its opposite—the determination to master new things and surmount challenges—lay in people's beliefs about why they had failed. People who attributed their failures to lack of ability, Dweck thought, would become discouraged even in areas where they were capable. Those who thought they simply hadn't tried hard enough, on the other hand, would be fueled by setbacks.*

I find it fascinating to learn that people who think their failures are due to their lack of ability or competency would be discouraged to push through the adversity even if they were, in fact, able and competent. The key word is if they *thought* they lacked ability. A

Individuals that have a fixed mindset believe success is achieved as a result of innate abilities.

"fixed mindset" is a belief that your abilities, intelligence, and talents are fixed traits. Individuals that have a fixed mindset believe success is achieved as a result of innate abilities. Failure is avoided at all costs and seen as unintelligent. The person strives for success to validate their intelligence.

A "growth mindset," explained by Dweck, *thrives on challenge and sees failure not as evidence of unintelligence but as a heartening springboard for growth and for stretching our existing abilities.* What if Heather Dorniden had simply given up after the public and undoubtedly humiliating fall? Would she have attributed her stumble to a lack of ability, losing her footing, and causing her to stumble? How would the outcome have changed if she had a fixed mindset? That tumble on the field fueled her desire to win even more. Unlike so many, Heather was motivated by her setback so much so that she ended up winning the race. She was less concerned, in my opinion, about looking smart, feeling embarrassed, or being criticized for her presumed clumsiness. She had a goal in mind—to finish the race and WIN! Had the outcome been different and she had lost, I believe that loss would have fueled her motivation to work harder, learn from that mistake, and do better the next time around. Dweck shares this sentiment, cited in the aforementioned Stanford article:

> *Students for whom performance is paramount want to look smart even if it means not learning a thing in the process. For them, each task is a challenge to their self-image, and each setback becomes a personal threat. So they pursue only activities at which they're sure to shine—and avoid the sorts of experiences necessary to grow and flourish in any endeavor. Students with learning goals, on the other hand, take necessary risks and don't worry about failure because each mistake becomes a chance to learn.*

Learning from the failures and applying what we learn becomes part of the success-attaining process.

Learning from failures and applying what we learn becomes part of the success-attaining process. Failures can push us to places we never thought we could reach. They demonstrate our courage and boldness, like in the example of Heather Dorniden. Failures are a matter of perspective, opening our eyes to what we can learn from the experience and what new skills we can gain because of them. Failures are nothing more than temporary setbacks that teach us, guide us, and point us in a new and better direction. Failures can be most motivating with a growth mindset.

Five Attempts – Four Failures = SUCCESS

In her 2013 TEDWomen Talk, Diana Nyad, record-setting long distance swimmer, gave a fifteen-minute talk about *Never Giving Up*. The sixty-four-year-old remarkable woman was the first person confirmed to swim from Cuba to Florida without the aid of a shark cage. This was her fifth attempt since 1978. In her talk, she shared with the audience about her experience making that 100-mile swim from Cuba to Florida. Amid jellyfish and choking on saltwater, she pushed herself and just kept swimming. Through hallucinations and a sea of pitch black, she pushed forward and just kept swimming. Diana had a lifetime goal that she achieved not after the first attempt, not after the second attempt, and not after the third and fourth attempt. She failed four times before achieving her goal. What would I ask Diana about overcoming four failures?

1) What did you learn in the four previous attempts that helped you succeed in this fifth attempt?

2) What was going through your mind after failing the first attempt? Did you see yourself as a failure? Did you consider giving up or even entertain the idea of quitting?

3) How difficult or easy was it to get back in the water after each unsuccessful attempt?

We become fixated on speeding up our efforts based on others' achievements and measure our success against theirs.

What a courageous and remarkable feat. Through her perseverance, Diana teaches us that success is not on a timeline or driven by deadlines. There is no set date or time when we will achieve success. Oftentimes, we become fixated on speeding up our efforts based on others' achievements and measure our success against theirs.

Perspective

As I mentioned previously, when I'm preparing for a presentation, I look for inspirational stories to share that will emphasize the point of my subject matter. In 2014, I came across this post on my social media page about an autistic boy who was given a test. I cannot be certain of the validity of this post, but the message came across loud and clear after reading. The instructions were to put five words in alphabetical order. At the very top of the page was the alphabet and below that were the five words:

apple   pumpkin   log   river   fox   pond

It was a seemingly simple task, but keep in mind that this boy was labeled autistic and therefore may have experienced challenges with this particular test. His response was quite amazing and shed new light on how we see things and whether what we see is right or wrong. His responses were:

alepp   ikmnppu   glo   eirrv   fox   dnop

Did you catch what he did? If you go back and reread the instructions, you might question whether or not he answered correctly. Perspective is an evaluation of facts from one person's point of view. Perspective

Perspective can change your outlook on your situation.

can change your outlook on your situation. Perspective prompts questions like these:

1) What other information can I gather from this situation?
2) Is there another way to view this problem, issue, or situation?
3) What positive aspects can I pull out of this experience?
4) Who else can I ask for objective feedback?

Getting input from an outside source can be beneficial when you're working through temporary setbacks. Trusted advisors, mentors, counselors, coaches, and friends can offer insightful and truthful feedback. We tend to be very critical of ourselves, so asking or rather inviting input from others can help us reassess the situation and look at it through different lenses. If you don't have a mentor or a person you trust, now might be the time to seek one out. Mentors are invaluable resources and offer a wealth of knowledge. We will explore more about mentors later in the book. Sometimes we need a swift kick in the pants to keep us from becoming quitters and doubt-creators. Surrounding yourself with doubt-creators will hinder your climb to success. Don't let people get in your ear about what may or may not be possible for you. I'm sure the people that rejected Steven Spielberg's application to attend film school had no idea of his true potential.

Rejection

Steven Spielberg is one of the most successful film directors of our time, directing high-grossing films such as Jaws, E.T. the Extra-Terrestrial, and Jurassic Park, to name a few. Several of his movies have won Academy Awards. Spielberg was the co-founder (with Jeffrey Katzenberg and David Geffen) of DreamWorks SKG, which they later sold to Paramount Pictures for an estimated $1.6 billion. He has an estimated net worth of $2.6 billion as of this writing. In November 2015, the influential filmmaker was awarded the Presidential Medal of Freedom, the nation's highest civilian honor. But like all good success stories, there was adversity that was the catalyst to his success.

Don't let people get in your ear about what may or may not be possible for you.

Long before Spielberg was a successful film director, he was rejected from film school—not once, but twice. He applied to USC's film school and was rejected because an admissions officer deemed his C-level average too low. He applied a second time and again was rejected. Are you noticing a trend with these success stories? **Failures often precede success**. This was nothing more than a temporary setback for Spielberg who knew that he was capable and did not doubt his abilities. He didn't have a fixed mindset, believing his talents were inborn, but he believed in a growth mindset that his temporary setback would be that spark to push him forward. Like Heather Dorniden and Diana Nyad, he had a goal in mind.

I had the privilege of meeting Steven, which is to say I served him food once while I was working in the mall. I didn't recognize him immediately. He approached the counter and placed his order.

As I was ringing him up, this nudging feeling inside of me kept saying, "I know this person from somewhere." But I couldn't put my finger on it. Was he an actor? Was he an entertainer? I couldn't let him walk away from my counter without asking him why he looked familiar. So I did, and the conversation went something like this:

Me: *Your face looks so familiar. Are you an actor?*

Spielberg: *No, I direct.*

Me: *Oh.*

Then it hit me. Embarrassing face emoji.

Talk about a making a BIG mistake. However, he was quite gracious when he walked away from my counter. I couldn't help thinking what he must've thought of me. *"Poor girl. She needs to get out more."* Now you may not have the privilege of meeting Steven Spielberg and engaging in a lengthy and invigorating conversation like me (lol), but let's imagine for a moment what he might say about overcoming rejection:

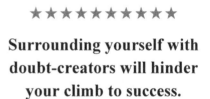

Surrounding yourself with doubt-creators will hinder your climb to success.

1) Rejection is a stepping-stone that gets you one step closer to a *yes*.
2) Rejection is a rehearsal, preparing you for the big day when you are doing exactly what you intended to do in spite of the setbacks.
3) Rejection thickens your skin and sharpens your resolve, making you a force to be reckoned with.

Strong resolve and a "can-do, will-do, must do" attitude will keep you fighting in the face of rejection.

Strong resolve and a "can-do, will-do, must do" attitude will keep you fighting in the face of rejection. Your attitude is your opinion about something and how you feel. It's in your body language, gestures, and what you say. Ridding yourself of negative (bad) words such as "I can't" or "I'm not" will help change your attitude about the things that are most important to you. Thinking negatively is just as bad. Negative thoughts begin occupying a space in your subconscious mind, and those thoughts begin to overshadow the good ones. You tend to focus on what you did, what you didn't do, or what you should have done. That pattern of thinking gradually pushes you into the defeated zone—a state of mind filled with doubt, self-pity, regret, and a give-up attitude.

Steven Spielberg didn't succeed as a top-grossing film director because he never faced failure. He succeeded because he made a choice to *fail forward*, using the film-school rejection as fuel for motivation. Failure is the new success if you choose to change your perspective.

Now Do This!

Scan the box below or type the URL into your browser and watch a short video of Tiana speaking on this topic. Select the video

"Failure Is the New Success"

https://www.youtube.com/tianaempowers

Chapter 3

Don't Quit. Get Bold.

"Freedom lies in being bold."
—Robert Frost

Malala is a global activist for girls' education and the 2014 Nobel Peace Prize recipient. She speaks out about the struggles for women in her native country of Pakistan and their right to education despite pushback, death threats, and an attempt on her life from "haters." Her resolve and fearless attitude is inspiring. What an accomplishment for this young adult and emerging leader, all before the age of eighteen.

Malala was born on July 12, 1997, in Pakistan. Named after a heroine in her country, she was raised to love learning. Her father ran a school close to their home and was an advocate for education in Pakistan. Her father became outraged about the restriction of education preventing girls from attending school. Malala clearly had an early introduction to advocacy and learned the importance of education from her father—an interest she would continue to pursue and speak about throughout her life.

In 2009 Malala started writing a blog under an alias describing fears she had about going to school and the restrictions for women in her country. Women were banned from watching television, banned from shopping, and banned from music. Despite the death threats she and her family received, Malala continued to speak out. She was later featured in a documentary, which also revealed her as the author of the blog. No longer protected by her alias, Malala became a vocal advocate, and in 2011, she was awarded Pakistan's first National Youth Prize. This news did not go over well with the Taliban, and it was said that they decided to kill her.

On her way home from school on October 9, 2012, Malala was attacked on a school bus. She was shot in the head, neck, and shoulder. Miraculously, she survived. Actually, she more than survived. She flourished! After a long recovery, she set up the Malala Fund in 2013, which advocates for girls seeking education. The Malala Fund brings awareness to the millions of girls that are being denied education and encourages them to lift up their voices to be heard. In 2014, she was the co-recipient of the Nobel Peace Prize. All of these things she accomplished before the age of eighteen. Now, what's your excuse?

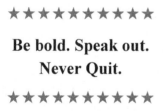

Be bold. Speak out. Never Quit.

Malala's story is a great one of standing up and stepping out. It's a story about not quitting and getting bold. Would anyone have blamed her if she stopped writing her blog or speaking openly about the issues with women's education in her country? How many of you would have quit after receiving death threats? She spoke confidently and boldly with a red target on her chest. She persevered and her story inspires us to be bold, speak out, and to NEVER QUIT!

Live Audaciously

Living audaciously is living boldly, bravely, fearlessly, daringly, and courageously. Do you think Malala lived audaciously? Let's check. Respond to each question with a yes or no or by placing a check next to the correct statement based on her story:

- Did she stand up for what she believed in?
- Was there imminent danger for her life, and did that danger hinder her from speaking out about what she believed in?
- Did fear stop her from writing about the disparities within education for women?
- Did she appear to have strong values from childhood that carried into adulthood?
- Did she continue to advocate for women's education after being shot in the head?
- Was writing a blog, speaking openly about education in her country, and being recognized for her work considered risky?
- Malala has contributed financially to women's rights for education.
- Malala is a great role model for men, women, and children all over this country.

Living audaciously means you may not be popular all the time. In fact, unpopular is your home address. Discomfort is your neighbor. By choosing to live audaciously, you choose to march to the beat of your own drum. You are daring to be

You are daring to be different and doing it unapologetically.

different and doing it unapologetically. No matter what people say and how disliked you are, you stay true to yourself and stay the course. There is a certain freedom and gratification that comes from living audaciously. It may not always be an easy road, but it is a gratifying one.

Reinvent Yourself

One of my favorite movies, aside from Superman, is Iron Man. That role, I believe, was meant for Robert Downey, Jr. He's charismatic, witty, and incredibly funny. According to the Hollywood Reporter, Iron Man 3 was the highest-grossing movie in 2013 with $1.2 billion in sales. However, before the success of Iron Man 3, Robert Downey, Jr. was struggling with his own personal villain—substance abuse. This struggle lasted for several years throughout his acting career. For the longest time, any time I heard his name I immediately associated it with trouble. Remarkably, in the midst of this dark time, his career flourished, especially with the Iron Man franchise. He reinvented himself and revitalized his career through that character. It was a radical change, and he came out wealthier and healthier (we hope) on the other side.

You don't have to be an actor, entertainer, or celebrity to reinvent yourself. Decide that you want to make a radical change and then do it. Here's how you start:

1. **Get clear with your "why."** Why is this change necessary? What will happen if I don't make this radical change today?
2. **Choose your happiness over someone else's**. Avoid making decisions to please others. It's a fact that you cannot please everyone, nor should that be your goal.
3. **Forget popularity, think unpopular**. Blend out, don't blend in with everyone and be ordinary. Who wants to be ordinary when you can be extraordinary?

I spent seven years in the financial industry and ten years in the retail industry working for someone else. When I had the revelation that I was no longer fulfilled by the work that I was doing, I decided to make a change. I started researching career paths and occupations based on my interests of training and speaking. I began to surround myself with individuals that were already doing the things that I wanted to do. *"If you want to have what others have, you have to be willing to do what others did to get what others have gotten."* I had to reinvent myself by rebranding

If you want to have what others have, you have to be willing to do what others did to get what others have gotten.

myself. In a 2014 article, *Brand It Like Apple,* I define branding and share seven key strategies to help you understand your brand and dare to get noticed:

Yes, you have a brand. Everyone has a brand that either attracts people to you or repels them from you. When they hear your name, see you in person or online, or read an article about you, they are associating you with a brand, a type of image or concept you represent. I once heard, "We all live in a brand-driven world, so if you don't have a strong position, you will go unnoticed." So, how do you strengthen your position? You employ the same techniques as Apple, the brand that speaks innovation, value, and game-changing technology without saying a word. The famous image of that perfectly shaped, slightly bitten apple has become the brand that represents technology and excellence. What does your brand say?

When I lost my job in 2011 and entered into the world of entrepreneurship, I was shifting my brand from "Bank Manager" to "Business Owner." For years, most people associated me with wealth management, lending, and financial advisement. But as that chapter closed, a new chapter was beginning in people development, management training, and coaching. So as my position in the marketplace shifted, I turned to Apple and began employing their techniques to communicate my new message and brand effectively. I learned how to shift my strategy from "think outside the box" to having no box at all. And it starts with...

Present a Total Package - *Apple products are simple, classic, and market well. From idea to implementation and from packaging to your pocket, Apple succeeds at presenting a total package. Is your brand aesthetically appealing and does it attract the right audience? How do you present yourself in the marketplace? Know your audience or your brand will suffer.*

Be Original and Think Beyond the Box - *Groundbreaking technology and inventive ideas have propelled Apple's brand into a class of its own. They excel at thinking beyond the box. Get rid of that old box altogether, recycle it if you must, but get rid of it. Creativity is the new standard. It has become the rule and not the exception.*

Let Others Market for You - *Word of mouth is a powerful and effective marketing tool. When a new iPhone is launching, where do you hear about it first? Positive WOM improves your reputation and creates "personal ambassadors" for your product or service.*

Typewriter Skills No More - *It's not enough to be skilled in a particular field. It's more important to have relevant skills that are in high demand. What do people want to buy? What do people need? Be niche-driven, dig deeper, and tap into your unique skills to find or, more importantly, CREATE the solution.*

iPad on Sale ...Think Again - *Have you ever seen an Apple product on sale on the website? Most companies have a "sale" section or tab on their site, but not Apple. The short answer is that they don't have to. Apple has placed a value on their product that* *does away with bargaining. They don't compromise and they consistently remain true to their products and customers. Your value is based on your skills and expertise. Don't compromise for a quick fix. People respect and appreciate value.*

*"**Game Changer**" - Are you playing the game or changing it? Strive for a blue ocean. Opposite of a red, bloody ocean which is saturated with competition, a blue ocean is untapped market space with little to no competition. Find your blue ocean.*

*"**Byte into an Apple**" – From "Think Different" to "The Internet in Your Pocket," brand slogans are just as powerful as the brand itself. When we hear a tagline or see a slogan, it incites an emotion or reaction. We instantly relate it to an image or experience, which can be positive or negative. A brand statement should encompass your value, proven results, and your promise.*

A poor brand is like a foul odor. It repels instead of attracting. It's like that person with bad breath that nobody wants to be around. And even if that person fixes the problem, they now have a reputation. Reputations are difficult to change from negative to positive.

A powerful brand is a sweet-smelling fragrance, pleasing to all the senses. It attracts the right audience and builds a loyal fan base for life. Strengthen your position and dare to be noticed.

Reinventing yourself by making a radical change doesn't mean you give up on who you are. It means repackaging what you have and presenting it in a different way to a different audience.

Stand Up and Step Out

Malala's story reminds me to stand up and be heard. It urges me to not hide in the shadows or cower behind fear. Her story encourages me to step out boldly from the shadows and emerge with fearlessness and confidence. It wasn't easy for her to take that stance. Can you imagine how difficult it was for her to be an enemy of the Taliban? Can you imagine how many times she had to look over her shoulder as she walked the streets of her neighborhood? Can you imagine how she must have felt with a gun pointed directly at her face and the hate on that man's face when he pulled the trigger? Yet amid all of that, she continued to speak out. She believes wholeheartedly that her message and her cause are worth the risk. Do you believe in something so passionately that you are willing to be criticized for it? Hated for it? Unpopular because you believe in it? There is a modern proverb of unknown authorship that reads, *"If you don't stand up for something, then you'll fall for anything."*

Now Do This!

Scan the box below or type the URL into your browser and watch a short video of Tiana speaking on this topic. Select the video

"Don't Quit. Get Bold."

https://www.youtube.com/tianaempowers

Chapter 4

Failures Make Us Great

"Only those who dare to fail greatly can ever achieve greatly."
—Robert F. Kennedy

I'm a professional failure with a degree in making mistakes and a masters in monumental misdirection. The "F" word can be intimidating and scary. It has a reputation of being associated with the wrong crowd. We use the "F" word with disgust, fear, and negativity. But I'm here to tell you the best-kept secret …

EVERYBODY HAS FAILED AT SOMETHING.

What we fail to realize, pun intended, are that failures often precede success. It's the growth part of the learning process. You are learning what works and what doesn't. Failures do three important things for us:

- TEACH us that we are human and capable of imperfection—a revelation some of us desperately need to help us recover from temporary setbacks and to guide us in a new direction.
- GUIDE us on a different path to avoid the mistakes already made and act as a compass to avoid future danger zones.
- POINT us in a new and better direction, revealing new ideas, new processes, and innovative strategies. Once we have been redirected and are on a new path, we must be motivated to take the next steps. Failures can MOTIVATE us.

In the next few pages, I'm going to share three stories that have shaped my view on the subject of failure. So now I ask, what do a basketball game, a failed marriage, and getting fired have in common? Keep reading and you'll find out.

Epic Fail

When I was in the ninth grade, I played for my high school girls' basketball team. It was my first time playing on a basketball team. We practiced every day after school for two hours, and I worked hard to develop skills that appeared to come so easily to the other players. Of course, that's not true. Nothing comes easy. I practiced dribbling the ball with my right hand and my left hand and in a seated position underneath my legs. I worked on my endurance, running sprints around the gym and doing "suicides," which involved running up to half court, up to the end of the court, and back multiple times. I worked on my right-hand layups and my left-hand layups. I worked on shooting the ball from anywhere on the court to the free throw line.

★ ★ ★ ★ ★ ★ ★ ★ ★ ★

Nothing comes easy.

★ ★ ★ ★ ★ ★ ★ ★ ★ ★

During one particular game against Beverly Hills high school, I experienced an epic fail. Beverly Hills wasn't exactly our rival, but whenever we played them, we always felt like we needed to bring our "A" game. We were the underdogs with newer talent and resided in a less affluent city. We had something to prove—or at least I did.

The game was close. We had taken the lead early on and had maintained it throughout the game, but by fourth quarter, Beverly Hills had caught up. It was in fourth quarter with less than a minute on the clock that I was fouled and had to go to the free-throw line and shoot two free throws. The game was tied and if I made these

36

two shots, we would have won the game; if I missed them, we would go into overtime.

I prepared to shoot the first free throw as I had practiced. I bent my knees, placed my fingers on the basketball with my elbows down by my side, and concentrated on using my legs as I came up to release the ball from my fingertips. The first shot went up … BRICK. I couldn't believe it. My confidence was shaken. It was confusing to me that I had missed, because earlier in the game I had shot and made two free throws. I prepared to shoot again, bending my knees, placing my fingers on the basketball with my elbows down by my side, concentrating on using my legs as I came up to release the ball from my fingertips. The second shot went up … BRICK! I glanced at my teammates on the bench, and I could almost feel the tears welling up in my eyes. I wanted to quit, run to the locker room, put my head in my lap, and cry my eyes out. Instead, I finished out the game, and we ended up losing in overtime.

On the bus ride home, other players on the team consoled me and tried to cheer me up. We were a team and, win or lose, we embraced it together. That experience taught me a lot about not giving up and wanting to quit. I failed at my two attempts and it hurt. I felt as though I let the team down. It was one game and I realized that it wasn't the end of the world. It was a moment that happened. It was also an experience that has shaped me into a person that sees these little stumbles as opportunities.

It was also an experience that has shaped me into a person that sees these little stumbles as opportunities.

Failures teach us, guide us, and point us in a new and better direction.

Failures...

- Build character
- Are momentary experiences
- Are not the end of the world

The Struggle Was Real

What do most twenty-two-year-olds think about? My guess would be enjoying life, hanging out with friends, preparing to graduate from college if that was part of their plan, and traveling. In a LinkedIn article published June 16, 2014 titled *#IfIWere22*, I wrote about my experience at the age of twenty-two and shared pearls of wisdom to the graduating class of 2014:

Unlike most of the graduating classes today, at age twenty-two I was already living out a very "adult" life. On February 28, 1998, I wasn't out partying with my gal pals or hitting the clubs, getting tipsy and "turnt-up." My college dorm wasn't filled with mementos from home and pictures of me, Mom, Little Junior and Sparky atop the armoire. I wasn't concerned about the latest iPhone or Samsung Galaxy, nor was I tweeting #thestruggleisreal. But, in fact, my struggle was very real.

At age twenty-two, I was working full time at a gourmet restaurant chain, managing a full staff of employees, celebrating my one-year wedding anniversary, and gaining weight because I was five months pregnant. #IfIWere22 again, what would I say to my younger self? Well, I can't turn back the hand of time, but I can move the dial forward and inspire you with these "teaching moments."

What do I know now that I wish I'd known then? Take my TIME and BE PATIENT. I always felt that there wasn't enough time, that I was on borrowed time, and I had to accomplish everything all at once—as though my life wasn't my own and I had to hurry up because time was running out. Patience is a virtue, but it wasn't mine at twenty-two. You don't need to rush and put enormous pressure on yourself to accomplish so much in a short period of time. Inventors and CEOs are getting younger and younger every year and I see the pressure that mounts on our young people. But give yourself time. Find out who you are and what you were born to do. Do you know what you want to be? Do you know your passion?

Am I where I thought I'd be? YES and NO. Honestly, I didn't give much thought to the future or my career. I was living in the moment trying to soak up everything. I dreamed of being a model, dancer, and choreographer. In college, I studied business and psychology but took dance on the side. It wasn't until about four years ago (which puts me in my mid-thirties for those of you trying to do the math) that I truly realized where I wanted to be in life— training, developing, speaking, writing books, and impacting lives in a real way. So, today I can answer with a resounding YES that I am exactly where I want to be. And it only took me thirty-four years to figure it out. It likely won't take you that long so keep calm and press on!

Advice I would give a younger person entering the workforce today: "Everyone wants to succeed, but not everyone is willing to do the work." This is a quote I recite often. Be willing to do the work. Get experience under your belt and embrace hard work. Find someone to be your mentor and listen more than you talk.

How did I get here? I said YES and took a leap of faith. I understood this concept way before Jim Carey's movie, Yes Man. When I was asked at age seventeen to become the manager over a full staff at a gourmet restaurant chain, I said, "YES. BRING IT ON." When I left my career in banking to pursue an entrepreneurial path, I said, "YES. I CAN DO THIS." When I was asked to speak to an audience for the first time, jitters and all, I said, "YES. I'M READY." When asked to write this article, sharing personal pieces of me and all my vulnerabilities to impact and influence your future, I said, "YES." What will you say YES to?

It took me a long time before I realized what I wanted to do with my career. A life lesson that I want to impress upon you is that there is no rush. Greatness doesn't happen overnight. Greatness takes time. Do you want to be good? Or do you want to be great?

Can you imagine being married at the age of twenty-two, working full time, and raising a child? Well, that was my life, but it was not the life that I had envisioned for myself at that age. At that age, you are still finding out who you are as a person,

I felt safe. And when we feel safe, that's usually an indication that we are getting too comfortable.

discovering what inspires you, and determining what you want out of life. When you invite someone else to be a part of your life, then it stops being about you and it becomes about *us*. As a young woman who was extremely independent and wanted to maintain her independence, I struggled with the "us" concept. Part of that struggle resulted in an early divorce. That wasn't the primary cause of the divorce, but it certainly added to the problems we faced.

Now, I am a happily married woman. My husband and I have been together for over thirteen years. I have learned that marriage doesn't mean that I have to give up who I am. I am simply sharing who I am with someone else. I had to learn a new language using words like "us," "we," and "our." That was

We look at other people's lives and situations and only see the "after" and not the "before."

a painful process. It's always painful when we are learning something new and changing our behavior to *do* better and *be* better. We look at other people's lives and situations and only see the "after" and not the "before." The after is the product of the before. People have come up to my husband and me and have said, *"You two make a great couple."* And, I would have to agree. Smiley face emoji. However, there was a "before," in another time and with another person.

Failure by Definition Is the Lack of Success

Married on Valentine's Day in 1998 and divorced on my birthday February 28, 2001—this was not exactly a picturesque ending to the story, but it is a true one nonetheless. It was a difficult time for me. Within a matter of three years, I went from being married to being a divorced single mother. How could I not feel like a failure? How could this not impact my self-esteem and confidence? I became depressed.

Depression can be toxic. The marriage was toxic, which is why I had to end it. Depression, however, is a different type of toxicity resulting from cause and effect. I got divorced, and it caused me to become depressed. The depression was a symptom of a self-inflicted illness. I was suffering from chronic "failure-itis." Yes, this is a word I made up, but it accurately describes my state of mind during this period. Failure by definition is the lack of success. *"I did not succeed in my marriage, therefore I have failed."* This is a dangerous state of mind that can lead to a cycle of poor choices and negative thinking. It wasn't until years later that I started to change my perspective and viewed the failed marriage as a blessing and life-saving experience. I started noticing small but significant changes about myself. I was happier, more at ease, and had peace of mind. I was experiencing a detox, cleansing my body and ridding it of toxins—toxic thinking, toxic people, and a toxic attitude. After several more months of "detoxing," I felt whole again. Renewed.

I changed my perspective and viewed the failed marriage as a blessing and life-saving experience.

Failures...

- Are not who you are but are something you have experienced. They are temporary, not permanent.
- Are not untreatable. Treat failures like a wound. They hurt at first and cause initial pain and discomfort, but after a while the pain ceases, the wound heals, and the scar becomes barely noticeable.
- Are about perspective. When you change your outlook, you can change your future outcome. A poor attitude will produce crap. A positive, action-focused attitude will produce a crop, a harvest of abundant possibilities.

Duck, and Come Up Swinging

It only took three words to change the trajectory of my career forever: "You are fired." In all of my years working, I have never been laid off from work, that is until May 2011. At the time, I was working in the financial industry, which I had

"Failure is about perspective. When you change her outlook, you can change your future outcome."

been doing for the last seven years. I was a regional manager for a retail banking credit union and responsible for overseeing the operations of five retail offices. I was promoted to this position within eighteen months of being at the company. I interviewed directly with the CEO and two other key executives. Ironically, during the interview the CEO asked, "Where do you see yourself in five years?" Without hesitation I replied, "Training and developing other people." Little did I know I was speaking my future career into existence.

From 2006 to 2009 the financial industry took a downturn. Companies were being bought out, and people were losing their jobs. It never occurred to me that I could be one of those people. I had a history of success and had never been terminated or laid off from a job. Other people around me in the organization were being laid off left and right, yet I was still there. Among this group of employees and managers, I was considered a veteran. My four years put me in the top tier group of my peers. Did I think I was untouchable? Not exactly. I had helped grow my offices, and I led the highest revenue-generating region in the organization. I received excellent customer service ratings and had good relationships and rapport with the people I worked with. I was nicknamed "the Golden girl" by a few of my close friends and colleagues. I felt safe. And when we feel safe, that's usually an indication that we are getting too comfortable. I'll expound on this idea of getting too comfortable later in the book.

It was early in the morning when I was making my way to the corporate office to meet with my supervisor. Just the day before, I was in the office and had packed up all of my belongings and taken them with me when I left that day. I knew what was coming. Call it a good feeling or intuition, but all of the signs were there. I walked into the office to be greeted by two people. I sat down and within a matter of five minutes, it was done. I took a breath, offered a few closing remarks, got up out of my chair, and politely walked out the door. I didn't cause a scene. I wasn't unprofessional. In fact, I was relieved. Truth be told, the work environment had changed and become more cutthroat. It felt more like high school with cliques, backstabbing, rumors, and gossip than a thriving financial institution.

When I arrived home after receiving the news that I was no longer employed with this company, I felt a great sense of peace wash over me. That night when I went to bed, I had the best sleep I had had in months. Within ninety days after leaving the company, I launched Tiana Sanchez Professional Coaching Services. An ambitious and bold move, wouldn't you say? When life throws you a punch, you duck and come up swinging.

Failures…

- Allow the truth to surface
- Can be motivating and give you the push you need
- Don't let you get too comfortable

Life experience is the best teacher. Allow my life experiences to teach you, guide you, and motivate you to see that quitting is not a sustainable option. Choose a "do-over." *Do over* so you can *do better*. And by doing better, you become a greater version of yourself.

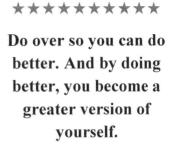

Do over so you can do better. And by doing better, you become a greater version of yourself.

When We Experience Failures, We...

When we experience failures, we have a tendency to react differently. I spoke on this very topic to a group of undergraduate students in northern California at a leadership conference. I asked the students to finish the statement, *"When we experience failures, we have a tendency to..."* Here are some of the responses received from the students:

- shut down
- shy away
- give up
- become depressed
- lose confidence
- get angry
- ignore our opportunities
- stay down
- doubt ourselves
- cry
- get mad
- discourage ourselves and others
- feel defeated

- stop
- get frustrated
- self-loathe
- feel disappointed
- stop pushing
- make decisions that in the long run will hurt us
- quit
- become stressed
- pull away
- stop believing in ourselves
- feel ashamed
- blame ourselves
- never move on
- run away

How many of you can relate to one or more of these responses? How many of you are experiencing some of these feelings right now? Several other students attending the same talk offered a different response to their experiences with failure:

- brainstorm
- find opportunities
- reassess the situation
- seek new opportunities
- rise
- learn
- give up or rise to meet the problem
- reevaluate
- be better
- keep pushing

It's clear that the lists are unbalanced. But this is true about life, isn't it? It didn't surprise me that there were more negative responses to how we experience failure than positive ones. It's important not to ignore those responses because it's how we feel in the moment. We must recognize what we are feeling and reflect by asking ourselves some important questions.

- Why did I fail?
- What did I or didn't I do?
- Was I given a second chance to change the outcome?
- What did I learn from that experience?
- What does this teach me?
- How will this guide me?
- How can this motivate me?

It's these last three questions that will move you from the first list to the second list and get you from being stuck in your feelings with a skewed view to changing your perspective and learning a new way to approach the "F" word. The "F" word can be intimidating and scary, but it doesn't have to be. I'm a professional failure with a degree in making mistakes and a masters in monumental misdirection and proud of it!

Now Do This!

★ ★ ★ ★ ★ ★ ★ ★ ★ ★

Scan the box below or type the URL into your browser and watch a short video of Tiana speaking on this topic. Select the video

"Failures Teach Us How to Be Great"

https://www.youtube.com/tianaempowers

★ ★ ★ ★ ★ ★ ★ ★ ★ ★

Chapter 5

The UPside of Change

Career & Life

"To improve is to change; to be perfect is to change often."
—Winston Churchill

Have you had an occasional misstep or stumble and lost your footing? You look around for something to hold onto to help you get your balance. If you're lucky, you find your balance and avoid the embarrassing tumble to the floor; otherwise hitting the floor is unavoidable. When things are changing around you, sometimes it feels like you're spinning, losing control, and unbalanced. Events occur in our lives that have a habit of changing the way we do things. Change is a disruption, a disturbance in the force. Change is unavoidable, and it causes us to rethink our motives, rethink our plans, and rethink our potential.

Change is unavoidable, and it causes us to rethink our motives, rethink our plans, and rethink our potential.

Rethinking Your Plans

Why do we struggle with change? Is it because it conflicts with our original plans? It's the part of us that yearns for stability and a sense of normalcy. We feel that what we have in place is good enough and that change is only going to make things more confusing. A good example of this would be my recent experience with getting a new printer.

My husband had been talking about getting a new wireless printer for about a year, but I turned down the idea because we already had a working printer in good condition. He argued that the new wireless printer would make things more convenient and easier for everyone in the household. We clashed on this idea for months because I could not see why we needed to change printers when we had a perfectly good printer.

So one day he just shows up with a new printer. I'm at home working at the computer, and my husband walks in with a big Epson box. He didn't say a word; he just sat the box on the counter. After a few minutes of silence, he

★ ★ ★ ★ ★ ★ ★ ★ ★ ★

Change is easier to accept when we understand the why and the benefits.

★ ★ ★ ★ ★ ★ ★ ★ ★ ★

proceeded to open the box, take out the printer, and assemble it. I pronounced aloud that I was not going to use this new printer. My plan was to continue using the old printer no matter what. I stuck to my guns for all of four hours. I was amazed at how I could print directly from my phone or send a fax through email. I no longer needed to connect my computer to the printer in order to print out documents. I could print a document from anywhere in the house. I was hooked immediately once I saw the benefits of convenience, and now I use the printer more than he does. I had to rethink my plans, and in doing so I now get documents printed more efficiently.

Change is easier to accept when we understand the why and the benefits. Change may not be easy, but it can be worthwhile when we clearly see the reward. Change, like failure, asks us to get a little uncomfortable. The discomfort of change may be temporary, but it doesn't mean it's less comfortable or less painful. How have you had to adapt to change in your life? What change did you resist in your career, life, or relationships? How are you better today because you embraced a radical change in your life?

We have all adapted to change. We may not like it, and sometimes it's not a choice. For example, when the law passed that banned texting and driving, we had to comply and adapt. We had to unlearn some behaviors. We didn't have a choice. We could no longer respond immediately to a text. We could no

The discomfort may be temporary, but it doesn't mean it's less comfortable or less painful.

longer send an email from the comfort of the driver seat. We could no longer tweet a message on Twitter because it could put our lives and someone else's life in danger. Did it make sense? Absolutely. Was it difficult for some of us to adapt to this change? Absolutely. We had to do away with old habits, learn and relearn a new set of skills. In order to deal with change effectively, find out the why and the reward.

Rethinking Your Potential

Twenty years ago, people would do well if they had a college degree; that was the goal, after all—go to college, get a degree, find a job, and make tons of money. Good plan, right? Times have changed, and that doesn't really describe the current career path for a twenty-first century professional. The current career path includes some version of that plan but leaves out critical steps. For example, some students don't make it to college. They start working right out of high school or while they are in high school. At some point, they may decide to go to college or trade school to gain more relevant skills that they can use on the job. They work their way up the career ladder, which leads to more opportunities, a promotion, and eventually more money. That's one scenario, and it could take several years to accomplish. The likelier and more preferred scenario is one that includes **mentorship, internships, work-based learning**, and **competency-based education**.

Mentorship—Get Lifted UP

Mentors are great resources for young adults and emerging leaders throughout life and career. A mentor is a subject matter expert in a specific field. They have "been there and done that." They are trusted advisors, and you can have more than one. Mentors provide sage advice, guidance, and direction. My first mentor was Ken Blanchard, renowned author and thought leader on everything leadership and management. Ken wrote the *One Minute Manager*, a new manager's Bible to understanding how to manage and lead

"Mentors are great resources for young adults and emerging leaders throughout life career."

others. As a "green" and unseasoned manager at seventeen, that book provided direction and helped make sense of this new role I was undertaking. It was life changing. It was career changing. Ken had managed to speak directly to me through that book, and I never forgot it.

In 2014, I met Ken Blanchard in person. I was in San Diego receiving leadership training for Situational Leadership II at the Ken Blanchard Company training site. Following the intense three-day training, each participant was invited to Ken's home for an intimate dinner and a fireside chat. In an article written in October 2014 and titled, *A Breakthrough Moment Sitting in Ken Blanchard's Living Room*, I describe my experience and the pearls of wisdom I walked away with:

Mega Author. Leadership Guru. Thought Leader. Ken Blanchard has written dozens of books, is a legend in the field of leadership, and remains a sought-after trainer on instructional systems across the globe. He has trained thousands through his proven methods on leadership, customer service, and management. Ken was my first mentor and coach, and he didn't even know it.

Twenty-one years ago in 1993, I began my career as a manager in a gourmet fast-food restaurant chain. I was clearly unseasoned in my new role and quite clueless. I was given a copy of the One Minute Manager *by Ken Blanchard, and my managerial lenses were refocused. That book made a huge impact on my career as a manager.*

During a brief trip to San Diego to attend Ken Blanchard's Situational Leadership course, I was honored to receive an invitation to meet my unofficially appointed mentor. After realizing I was going to have an opportunity to meet Ken

Blanchard and his wife at their home, I searched and searched for my original copy of the One Minute Manager *for Ken to sign. I took drastic measures and even recruited my husband to do a thorough search of the garage, but at the end of our search, we came up empty-handed. It occurred to me that in my fifteen years in management, somewhere along the way I passed on those words of wisdom—that once inspired me—to some unassuming young manager and aided them, no doubt, in their development. Isn't that what a good manager does—share knowledge as a way of paying it forward to up-and-coming managers? I think Ken would agree.*

Seated in the living room with a copy of Great Leaders Grow *in one hand and a glass of Pinot Grigio in the other, I listened intently as Ken shared stories from the experience of losing his first home of twenty years to working with various leaders at top companies. He offered up advice on sustaining a long and happy marriage, speaking openly about his marriage with wife, Margie. But what stood out the most was his gentle, kind, and sharp wisdom. During those sixty minutes with Ken and Margie, I learned about providing meaningful work for our young leaders, servant leadership, leadership responsibility, and workplace integrity. Learn. Teach. Inspire.*

Advice to Millennials: seek out mentorship. *Encourage the up-and-coming leaders to take on a "we" not "me" approach and mindset. Focus on the collective effort of the team. Develop millennials by getting them involved in work at the organizational level as well as meaningful work that will have a direct impact on the world.*

Servant Leadership *is about helping your employees get an "A" in performance. By providing clear goals and frequent coaching* *and feedback, employees are more engaged. The accountability for this level of clarity and follow up is the responsibility of the manager.*

"Integrity Communication" is a term Ken adopted when working with an executive from Cold Stone Creamery. "You don't talk about anyone if they're not there." This was the first time I had ever heard of integrity communication in all my years of management. It's a rule we foolishly hope all people adhere to, but it's not always practiced. What a difference this could make in organizations if integrity communication became part of the value and culture.

Wise advice for anyone with an ear to listen. The breakthrough moment came when leaving the Blanchard home.

NEVER STOP LEARNING no matter your age.

NEVER STOP TEACHING especially to anyone who is brave enough to listen.

NEVER STOP INSPIRING because you may be planting a seed in someone's life. And if you're blessed enough, you might even get to see the fruit of that seed.

This is the impact that one mentor can have on your life. A mentor can be a community leader, an athletic coach, a pastor, a supervisor, a CEO, a trusted friend, and just about anyone who is willing to accept the role of mentor. A great mentor is someone who has already

A great mentor is someone who has already reached a level of success that you are trying to attain or is in a particular field you are pursuing.

reached a level of success that you are trying to attain or is in a particular field you are pursuing. Mentors can help you bring clarity to your career path. They challenge you to find your *own* path—not what others deem as a suitable career path. They help you to rethink and realize your full potential.

Internships—Get Skilled UP

Internships are potential-sparking roles. Internships get your foot in the door at a company and provide you with much-needed work experience. There are paid and unpaid internships. When deciding on the right internship, weigh all of your options before saying no to an unpaid internship. Although you may not see the rewards upfront, the payoff could be quite substantial.

Internships often lead to permanent placement within the organization. It's an informal trial period for you and for them. In that time, you have the opportunity to allow your skills to shine through and show them your unique capabilities. It's also a time to learn and be a sponge, absorbing as much as you can for as long as you can. It's a time to build up your network of professional contacts and make meaningful connections. A meaningful connection with the right person can change your life. The right connection can lead to greater career opportunities. Internships allow you to get on-the-job work experience that is so desperately lacking in young adults and emerging leaders.

Work-Based —Get Worked UP

Work-based learning is part of the on-the-job experience. Its effectiveness lies in the connection between what people learn in training and their ability to apply it on the job—learning and applying what was learned. But when you are learning a new skill, you will stumble. A few things to note about training:

- Training must be relevant to one's role and position within the company.
- Trainees must be given an opportunity to increase their knowledge and develop skills that are relevant to their career.
- Trainees must be allowed to fail and must be allowed a "do over."

Work-based learning could include job shadowing and internships. Imagine that you are given an opportunity to learn and practice what you learned without the fear of repercussions. Would you apply more effort? Would you do better? Would you be better prepared to do the work? I've spoken with many professionals whose companies do not provide structured training yet set high expectations for performance. Are they setting them up for success? Or are they setting them up for failure?

Competency-Based Education—Get Built UP

According to the US Department of Education, competency-based education, competency-based learning, and personalize Learning *"provide flexibility in the way that credit can be earned or awarded, and provide students with personalized learning opportunities."* The flexibility focuses not only on the learning

The idea that you need experience coupled with education changes the way young adults and emerging leaders approach a profession.

part but also on *demonstrating* what was learned. Students prove they are capable and have the knowledge and skills to receive credit

for learning. In other words, getting an 'A' on an exam or passing a test simply won't do. Telling you I can drive a car without showing you my license is not enough. The student has to be able to demonstrate the skill in order to receive credit. It's another way of saying that you need experience under your belt. The idea that you need experience coupled with education changes the way young adults and emerging leaders approach a profession.

The Crappy Skills Gap

Young adults and emerging leaders are now faced with the task of not only obtaining a four-year degree but also honing in on critical skills needed to secure a good-paying job. I can give you statistics filled with numbers and percentages to make this point, but here's what you need to know. Employers have candidly shared that some of the skills students learn in school are not transferable to the work environment. They call it a skills gap—a job or position that requires a certain set of skills that the applicant does not possess. It's a little frightening to think that you spent four years in college and that when you graduate you may not land the job of your dreams. Do you want to know why?

Aside from having technical savvy, basic job skills, and motivation to do the work, leadership skills are one of the top sought-after skills for employers. In the 2012 report, *Bridging the Skills Gap*published by the American Society for Training and Development (now the Association for Talent Development—ATD), this skills gap is broken down from an employer's perspective:

In addition to industry skills gaps, employers are observing a lack of critical soft skills—such as communication, collaboration, creativity, and critical thinking—in today's workforce. These soft skills continue to exist even with the US's persistent unemployment, according to The Skills Gap: Reversing Washington's Lack of Skilled Workers Through Early Learning. *In a 2010 survey of 2,000 executives conducted by the American Management Association, nine in ten executives said these enhanced soft skills are important to support business expansion, but less than half of those executives rated their employees as above average in those skills.*

In a member survey, respondents were asked, *"What are the specific skills gaps that your organization is experiencing now?"* The leadership skills gap surpassed technical skills, sales skills, and project management skills. So, why is there such a gap, and how does one get leadership skills when they're sitting behind a computer all day interacting with people via text message and spending hours upon hours online?

Leadership skills come from interaction with other people. It's a learned skill that is demonstrated by the act of doing. Advances in technology have become, in my opinion, a double-edge sword. On the one hand, it has provided smarter technology, innovation, and more efficient processes. On the other hand, it has taken away some jobs that were once run by people and now run by computers. It has in some ways taken away the element of human touch and has made us dumb. Now I will speak for myself on that last point, although I'm sure some of you reading this can relate. Let me give you an example.

It would take me a long time to recall the last instance when I actually punched in a phone number to call one of my friends. Don't get me wrong. I make calls; I just don't have to physically type in the number to do so. All I have to do is simply look up the contacts icon on my smartphone, find the person's name, and hit send. This may seem like something of little importance, but let's dissect this a bit further. My ability to recall numbers has slowed down because I don't practice this skill. I wouldn't call it memory loss—more like a lack of mental strength training. When an athlete gets injured and stops working out for months and months, and those months turn into years, the muscles weaken. They become frail and lose the ability to function as well as they did before the injury. When you don't practice a skill, you lose it. Period. This is worth repeating. When you don't practice a skill, you lose it!

★ ★ ★ ★ ★ ★ ★ ★ ★ ★

When you don't practice a skill, you lose it. Period. This is worth repeating. When you don't practice a skill, you lose it.

★ ★ ★ ★ ★ ★ ★ ★ ★ ★

Another example is the social network. Yep, I went there. According to a report done by Common Sense Media—a nonprofit focused on helping children, parents, and educators navigate the world of media and technology—tweens and teens spend an average of nine hours a day on social media. That's longer than a standard workday, time we don't get to spend talking to one another face-to-face and time we don't get back. Spending time in the presence of others helps build social and interpersonal skills. There is a difference, contrary to what some of you may believe, between talking with someone over the phone and talking with someone in person. Are major business deals done over the phone? It's highly unlikely. It's difficult to build trust without looking a person in the eye. You are unable to look at the person's body language, see their facial expressions, and get a real sense of who they are and how they feel. That comes from a real and genuine face-to-face interaction. Spending nine hours a day and approximately 3,285 hours a year on social media, I'm not surprised there's a skills gap.

Have you heard of FOMO? FOMO is defined as *anxiety that an exciting or interesting event may currently be happening elsewhere, often aroused by posts seen on a social media website.* Wait, what?! There is a new breed of followers, tweeters, and social media fanatics that have caused the development of a new disorder. Really? This is a wake-up call for us to ask ourselves, *"What are we really missing out on?"* I was at the post office recently, standing in line waiting for the doors to open, and I heard a woman who was three people behind me make a comment about how no one in line was talking to each other. She was an older woman and obviously had lived in a different era when people talked to one another. Imagine that.

Change is a disruption, a disturbance to our sense of normalcy. It causes us to rethink our motives, rethink our plans, and rethink our potential. The upside to change is embracing something

★ ★ ★ ★ ★ ★ ★ ★ ★ ★ ★

Change is a disruption, a disturbance to our sense of normalcy.

★ ★ ★ ★ ★ ★ ★ ★ ★ ★ ★

different. That something different might lead to something better. Don't let years of doing something one way hinder you from trying something new. The lesson in this chapter is that change can be a disruption with tremendous value.

Now Do This!

Scan the box below or type the URL into your browser and watch a short video of Tiana speaking on this topic. Select the video

"Change Is Inevitable"

https://www.youtube.com/tianaempowers

Chapter 6

Unleashing Your Inner Champion

"Everything you want is on the other side of fear."
— **Jack Canfield**

In June 2013, Warner Bros released Man of Steel, the latest movie version of Superman. It blew me away! It's the good old-fashioned story of the good guy versus the villain, and the villain is defeated! Of course, the special effects did not disappoint, but it was the way the story was told that stuck with me. The forces behind the film told the story in such a way that helped me better understand Superman's character, his journey to greatness, and rise to HERO status. In my opinion, this version told the story better than any of its predecessors.

Whether we grew up reading the comic books or watching a black and white episode on the tube, we were entranced with Superman and his power to conquer. George Reeves, the original Superman, Christopher Reeves, Brandon Routh, or most recently Henry Cavill as the Man of Steel—we enjoyed them all. So, why is it that we gravitate toward a hero who champions over adversity? Is it because we enjoy the thrill of a good fight? Do we see a parallel in our own lives? Is it because it gives us that feeling of hope? Heroes and champions, I believe, represent something we deeply desire to

We may not wear a red cape, but some of us are certainly heroes in our own right.

be. Courageous. Strong. Resilient. We may not wear a red cape, but some of us are certainly heroes in our own right.

A Champion Is Alive in You

A champion is a defender, a supporter, and a victor. Your inner champion is your resolve and unique character trait that propels you forward in the face of adversity. Beneath the surface and behind the fear, there is a champion alive in you. Yes, I said fear. We experience fear in our life. In fact, I believe there are four types of fear that we experience and that we need to push through in order to reveal that inner champion within us. In the book *Undefeatable: Conquering Self-Defeat*, I describe these four types of fears in chapter three. Let's revisit these four fears.

(1) Fear of Failure

Here is the hard truth that I want you to know. YOU WILL EXPERIENCE FAILURES. If you can grasp that concept today, you will take one giant leap in removing that fear of failure. It's amazing to me how children don't fear failure. Children will fall down and get right back up without hesitation, worry, or concern. They dust themselves off and figure out a way to avoid the fall next time. They don't spend time thinking about the **fall** but focus more on succeeding at standing or walking or running. If we focus more of our attention on the outcome (the goal) and spend less time concerned about the fall (the failure), we might find ourselves achieving the goal quicker.

(2) Fear of Taking Risks

I believe in taking calculated risks. There is a difference between doing something on a whim and doing something with careful thought and consideration. It's important to weigh the pros and the cons, the advantages and the disadvantages, before taking risks. As an entrepreneur, there are many risks that you take. But for those who succeed and those who do not, I believe the difference is in the type of calculated risks they took. If we don't take risks, we will become stale, stagnant, and normal. Who wants to be normal? Taking risks is a belief in possibilities.

Sometimes taking a risk simply means doing something that feels abnormal, unfamiliar, and scary.

Risks are taking a leap of faith even though you cannot be entirely certain of the outcome. Think about all the inventors, artists, musicians, and people in our history that decided to take a risk on an idea, a concept, or dream. Sometimes taking a risk simply means doing something that feels abnormal, unfamiliar, and scary. It could take on the form of applying for a position where you have little experience. It may look like asking someone you like on a date knowing that there could be rejection that follows. It could be investing in a new venture without the certainty of the market. It's putting all of your vulnerabilities out there for everyone to see.

To overcome this type of fear, learn to take calculated risks. Don't avoid taking risks altogether, but be decisive in your risk-taking and take a leap of faith.

(3) Fear of Greater Responsibility

Teachers, parents, business owners, supervisors, and people with authority and great responsibility may experience this type of fear. It is the fear of being accountable and responsible for someone other than yourself. That level of accountability can be overwhelming and make someone feel as though they're inadequate and ill- equipped to take on that greater responsibility. I ask people that experience this type of fear, *"Is it a fact or is it an opinion?"*

To accept the weight of an entire country on your shoulders is one heck of a responsibility, yet a select few have successfully managed that obligation. Every president of the United States has accepted that responsibility. How much more can you take on? Are there people counting on your leadership? Step up! Take yourself out of the picture and think of the other individuals that are counting on you.

(4) Fear of the Unknown or Uncertainty

What we don't know scares us. Some of us (pointing the finger at myself) like being in control. Some of us would like to know step-by-step what's going to happen, when it's going to happen, and how it's going to happen. Those questions can haunt someone who likes to be exact about details. Some things, however, are unpredictable. We simply cannot predict every outcome. That level of uncertainty makes people like me crazy. Taking risks can be frightening. There is no definite predictor of success. Our skepticism causes hesitation and instead of doing something, we do nothing, which

★ ★ ★ ★ ★ ★ ★ ★ ★ ★

Don't avoid taking risks altogether, but be decisive in your risk-taking and take a leap of faith.

★ ★ ★ ★ ★ ★ ★ ★ ★ ★

is actually doing something. Did you get that? Doing nothing is doing something. When you find yourself doing nothing, you need to step outside of the situation and ask yourself, *"How flexible am I willing to be in this situation? What adjustments can I make to keep things in perspective?"*

The ability to overcome these types of fear is to recognize when your fear stops you from taking action or making an important decision. Fear, like failure, is information. Use this information to understand what might be

A champion has tenacity and is able to withstand a certain level of discomfort.

holding you back from unleashing your inner champion. A champion has tenacity and is able to withstand a certain level of discomfort. Discomfort, you will soon find out, is not a bad thing at all.

Sitting in Your Discomfort

Are you ready to run for the hills? Don't start running just yet. In fact, take a seat. Are you comfortable? Good. Relax. Prop your feet up and get real comfy. I'm officially giving you permission to get comfortable. I want you to remember this feeling of comfort and relaxation. If you have a lounge chair at home, go sit in it. Recline the seat back and close your eyes. Feeling comfortable yet?

When we are too comfortable, we lose our edge, our sharpness. We become stagnant and tolerant of our current situation. This can be dangerous. I want you to be aware of the different levels of comfort that you may experience or have experienced. To illustrate this point, I will liken the levels of comfort to different types of chairs.

The Lounge Chair—Inaction

Well, you've already experienced this chair if you followed my instructions at the beginning of this section. The lounge chair is the state of mind where you have no worry, no concern, and are in a complete state of relaxation. It feels good here, and therein lies the danger. A comfy chair can be hard to get out of mentally and physically. The lounge chair doesn't challenge you; it simply keeps you as you are. It offers you the amenities of good living and comfort. There are no risks here, no real fear. But when you sit too long in the lounge chair, you lose your mobility. If you find yourself sitting too long in this chair, get up quickly to avoid getting stuck.

The Desk Chair—Tolerance

Now the desk chair that I'm referring to is one of the old school desks we had back when I was in grade school, circa 1980s. There is one way to enter the desk and one way to exit. The chair resembled an upside down "h" if you were sitting in the chair. It was confining and restricting, which made it difficult to move around. This chair was hard and uncomfortable. It offered little back support and one could get fidgety sitting in this chair too long. This most certainly was not one of my favorite chairs to sit in but, like you, I tolerated this mild discomfort while in grade school. Eight hours a day, five days a week, nine months out of the year. Why did we do it? Well, one could surmise that we really didn't have much of a choice. Those were the standard desk chairs and everyone had to comply. One could also conclude that the discomfort was tolerated because

The discomfort was tolerated because we were there for a larger purpose...

we were there for a larger **purpose**—our education. We tolerated this discomfort because we were instructed to do so. We tolerated this discomfort because we knew it was temporary. We tolerated this discomfort because we understood the *why*. Unleashing that inner champion in you means that sometimes you will have to sit in your discomfort and endure a certain level of pain and uneasiness to obtain a greater reward.

Unleashing that inner champion in you means that sometimes you will have to sit in your discomfort and endure a certain level of pain and uneasiness to obtain a greater reward.

Toddler's Chair—Ego

Have you ever sat in a toddler's chair? These miniature-sized adult chairs sit low to the ground but only for adults. To a child, they are the perfect size. For an adult, they make you feel like Alice in Wonderland. You've fallen down the rabbit hole, and everything has shrunk ten sizes. Knees are up to your chest, and your arms are hanging low to your side and are close to touching the ground. Imagine a six foot six male adult sitting in a toddler chair. Is this even possible? Think about this for a moment. I want you to get a visual of how uncomfortable this person might look and feel. How might this person look engaging in a conversation with someone who is in a standing position? This person might feel belittled, talked down to, and awkward. It's a humbling experience, not just an uncomfortable one.

Humility is part of a champion's DNA, or at least it should be. If you find yourself in the toddler's chair state of mind, take note and find out why. Have you let your ego get the best of you? Are you relishing your accomplishments so much so that you have forgotten

Ego, self-absorption, and a haughty attitude will cause uneasiness and distress.

to be humble? Ego, self-absorption, and a haughty attitude will cause uneasiness and distress. This level of discomfort is a red flag for people who do not take direction from others well and who are not receptive to feedback. Is this you? Ouch!

Swivel Chair—Distraction

The swivel chair is probably the most fun and entertaining chair. It doesn't appear to be an uncomfortable chair, so we take a seat. It spins, rotates, and pivots. It's like being on a roller coaster ride. You feel the exhilaration and excitement with each turn. You get a 360° view with one spin. You can stop at any given point, giving you a unique vantage point of your surroundings. You don't miss a beat. You can change direction and adjust your seat up or down to your specifications. Oh, what fun it is to ride! But all that spinning can make you dizzy. Are you spinning out of control—literally? Have you lost your **focus**? Are you feeling unstable and lost? Planting your feet on the ground gives you **stability**.

Is this your state of mind? If you're seated in this chair, you may feel unstable, insecure, and unfocused. It's okay to take a ride now and then, but pace yourself. Learn how to put on the brakes and plant your feet on the ground. Stop if you find yourself becoming distracted by the bells and whistles of the swivel chair. Refocus. The discomfort you experience in this chair is losing focus. You become distracted and lose sight of your purpose and mission.

Director's Chair—Leadership

Leading. Managing. Instructing. Organizing. Guiding. Mentoring. Counseling. To put it in simpler terms, this is the state of mind where you are running things! You have a plan and you're executing that plan. You are in complete control and rely on your skills, wit, and experience. You are respected and looked upon as an expert in your field. You can make decisions quickly and make a course correction if need be to get back on track. You lead with integrity and carefully consider all options before making a decision that will not only impact you but others. You live by the code of shared success yet take full responsibility when the chips are down.

A director's chair moves where you move. It folds, it bends, and it's flexible. Change does not frighten you—it empowers you. You see change and you see possibilities. You embrace your imperfections, but you continuously work on improving yourself. You believe that if everyone wants to succeed, then everyone has to be willing to do the work. There comes a time when you have to pass the baton and pass on that shared knowledge. This is not a seat of discomfort but a seat of leadership, which can by its own definition be uncomfortable. The fear of greater responsibility can cause someone seated in this chair to doubt themselves, their skills, and their abilities. If you're not ready to lead, you're not ready to be a champion.

This is not a seat of discomfort but a seat of leadership, which can by its own definition be uncomfortable.

Kick Defeat to the Curb

You will experience failures in your life, but that does not mean you have to become defeated by them. Failure is a temporary setback when one has not achieved an expected outcome or result. Defeat, on the other

Defeat is becoming overwhelmed by the failure, wallowing in self-pity, and quitting.

hand, is being overwhelmed by the failure, wallowing in self-pity, and quitting. Overcoming defeat means activating your drive, ambition, and boldness. Overcoming defeat means admitting to yourself that you are not perfect and that your imperfections are what make you unique. Overcoming defeat means seeing the situation with different lenses and changing your perspective.

I want you to do an activity with me. I want you to get out a piece of paper and draw a box. In that box I want you to draw two lines so that there are three columns. In the first column, I want you to write the word *failure* at the very top. In the second column, I want you to write the word *losses*. And in the third column, I want you to write the word *wins*. Failures will reflect anything that you pursued but did not achieve. Failures may also reflect a temporary setback that you experienced.

Losses will reflect something that you no longer have in your possession. That can be something tangible or intangible. The loss may also reflect something that you needed to kick to the curb anyway. Here's yet another example to help you better understand losses, courtesy of my life experiences.

After my divorce at the age of twenty-five, I struggled to find meaning in that relationship. It caused me tremendous grief and pain in the beginning. I thought about the fragility of my then three-year-old son and how he would be impacted. It tore into my confidence as a parent as well as my self-worth. I would lie in bed all day and all night. When I would wake up, I would take sleeping medicine, no matter the time of day, to relax me and keep me asleep. I was a private person and spared my family and friends the drama of my troubles. Truthfully, I was embarrassed. I was knee-deep in defeat and going deeper. And then it happened. I heard a little voice that was familiar to me and calling my name, "Mommy." An innocent and precious little person was counting on me. My son was counting on me to be present. He was counting on me to guide him. He was counting on me to be Mom.

Failures	Losses	Wins

Losses can be a blessing if what you lost was causing you more harm than good. The truth of the matter was that the marriage was toxic and causing me more harm than good. The truth is children are resilient as described in chapter one. He was going to be ok if I was ok. The truth is support and reassurance are vital for a defeated person. My decision to "spare" my friends and family was well intentioned but misguided. Finally, I realized the biggest truth of them all: this was a loss I would happily take again. Smiley face emoji.

Wins describe achievement, successes, and accomplishments. Wins may also reflect a positive attitude in the face of adversity. Not giving up after experiencing a temporary setback would be a win in my book. This exercise is about reflection and getting in touch with your feelings and your reactions to different situations. Once you have a better understanding of how you react, then you can change how you respond in the future. For each word, I am going ask you to respond to three questions. For example, let's take failure. In the failure column in your box, I want you to think about a situation where you failed. It could be a recent situation or something that happened a long time ago. What did the failure look like? What did it sound like? And how did it make you feel?

What did the failure look like? (Describe the situation in detail.)

- Did it look like unemployment?
- Did it look like a breakup?
- Did it look like an investment gone bad?
- Did it look like a poor relationship with a family member?

What did it sound like? (What did you hear others say or what did you say to yourself?)

- "You're fired."
- "I want to break up."
- "You're failing this class."
- "I'm so disappointed in you."
- "I'm such a loser."

How did it make me feel? (Describe personal feelings and emotions.)

- discouraged
- inadequate
- frustrated
- motivated

The feelings you describe may not be negative. That's ok. Write down how you felt. Do this for all three words and ask yourself the same questions. Complete this in a quiet place where you have time to think and reflect without distraction. Remove yourself from any judgment or initial self-critique. Sometimes we refrain from being totally honest for fear of what someone else might have to say or because it's hard admitting to ourselves our own weaknesses. No judgment. No self-critique for now.

Now that you've made your list, this next step is a very important one. Take that list and look it over very carefully. Were you honest with your responses? Did you notice any pattern of emotions? Were the columns balanced? Which category was overflowing with examples? After you look it over and answer the questions honestly, throw it in the trash. This is not a pity party or an exercise to keep you stuck in the past. You might ask, *"Get rid of the wins too?"* The wins are motivational **reminders** of what you can achieve. If you need to be reminded, do the exercise again. Do it as many times as you like until you are assured that your failures and losses will not defeat you! Use the following acrostic of DEFEAT to help you.

D   **Decide** to change your outlook. Make a conscious decision to alter your perspective in unfavorable situations. Is a loss really a loss if what you lost did more harm than good? You have a choice to either be an overcomer or to be overcome by defeat.

E   **Embody** a superhero attitude. Put on the figurative red cape and run toward problems, not from them. Attack the problems head on. It will be frightening. It will be uncomfortable. But you get stronger by getting uncomfortable.

F   **Fail** forward into the future and avoid failing backwards into the past. It happened. Now what? What will you do to move forward and achieve the outcome you desire? What is your action plan? Do you need a new approach? Failing forward is looking ahead to what you need to do—not behind to what you should have done.

EAT   "Eat the Frog." Disgusting, right? Eating the frog means doing the task that you despise the most, first. Why do we procrastinate on getting things done? Why do we avoid the things that make us uncomfortable? You should have a pretty good idea by now about why we choose comfort over discomfort. The "frogs" in your life might be making a big change, letting go of something you hold dear, saying yes to something, or saying no to someone. It's that one thing that you know you need to do, but you will do everything in your power to avoid it. So, my advice to you: EAT THAT FROG! You won't like it, but do it anyway.

There is work that you need to do. There are questions that you need to answer. Are you bold and confident when facing any challenge or obstacle? Are you motivated when the going gets tough? Are you alright with getting uncomfortable? Are you ready to be honest with yourself? Are you ready to understand what fear has been holding you back and why? Do you know what seat you've been sitting in too long, and are you ready to change seats? Do you see yourself as a victor in any area of your life? Start calling yourself a winner before, during, and after the outcome. It's your attitude and state of mind that will kick defeat to the curb for good!

Now Do This!

Scan the box below or type the URL into your browser and listen to a podcast of Tiana being interviewed on Failure & Sitting in Your Discomfort

https://nolimit2yoursuccess.com/talks/

Chapter 7

F'd UP and Ballin

An Athlete's Story by Tian M. Daniels

"I'm looking for activity. I put players in and take them out based on effort and defense, not making or missing shots."
—Doc Rivers

Win or lose, you never stop ballin. Ballin is living the good life, having it all. There is another definition that applies to basketball, which means playing ball and playing it well. You may win some games and lose some games, but never stop ballin—playing full-out, giving 100 percent effort and 100 percent attitude. Doc Rivers, head coach of the LA Clippers, once said, *"Sometimes you will hate me because I will tell you the truth about your game. And the truth can hurt/humble you."* And to that I say, let the truth set you free!

Ballin on the Court

In high school, I played organized basketball. I was a point guard, the person taking the ball down the court and directing the plays. As co-captain, I was responsible for motivating the other players and setting a good example through my leadership. As much as I loved basketball, it took a backseat when it came to academics. As a student-athlete, a student who plays a sport while also maintaining good grades, I juggled a lot of things. Academics always came before athletics. This was a priority.

I decided to play basketball because I was passionate about the game and playing it. Not only that, I understood the amount of doors it could open up for me in college and beyond. There are three things that helped me succeed in class and on the court: *work ethic, drive,* and *skill development.* A strong *work ethic* is vital if you want to have any success. Work ethic is your moral code, a set of principles that you work by. *Drive* is your get-up-and-go attitude that pushes you to be better and do more. Drive is necessary when pursuing anything in which you wish to excel. Work ethic and drive alone do not produce success. At the end of the day your skills, know-how, and abilities are what you need. *Are you capable to do the work? Do you know how to do the work? Are you able to do the work?*

Playing a sport has taught me many things about ups and downs. In sports, you will almost always experience failure or a loss at least once. Whether it was a missed goal, a turnover, or a dropped pass, failure is inevitable. I remember the first time I lost a game. After losing, I didn't want to talk to anyone. I was angry because we lost and frustrated because I knew I could do better. I was able, capable, and had the skills to help my team win.

Losing, as we learned in the previous chapter, can be viewed differently if we change our negative mindset to an optimistic mindset. A loss points out areas where you need to improve and grow. When you lose, you are able to learn from the mistakes that caused your loss and ultimately grow from them. I hate to lose more than I love to win, but I love to improve more than I

I hate to lose more than I love to win, but I love to improve more than I hate to lose.

hate to lose. Translation: Winning matters, but if I lose and can learn from my mistakes to do better, then that ultimately means more to me than the win.

Losses and failures can be discouraging, but when a win shows up, it's a sweet victory. When you excel at anything, it is very easy to have a positive mindset and look forward to what's next. In our culture, winning is used as motivation to get more wins. *"Do what you did before, and you will surely get a win,"* we might say. But what if a player plays better

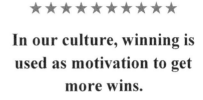

In our culture, winning is used as motivation to get more wins.

than you, shoots better than you, and passes better than you? Will the same strategy work? You have to rethink your strategy. Don't get me wrong, winning a game is the best feeling ever! You feel untouchable. The win feels especially good when people come up and tell you that you played well and say, *"Good game, man."* But what encourages me to do better is when we lose and someone says, *"Even though you lost the game, you never gave up and played full-out until the last buzzer."* Now, that's encouraging.

Ballin in Class—Real World. Real Struggles.

Will playing sports and applying what I learn in school help me in the real world? This is a question I often ask myself. As a young adult, it's important to take your education seriously. Don't "F" up! I love playing ball, but if I choose not to play professionally, or suffer a game-ending injury, my education will prove very beneficial. The answer to that first question, of course, is YES! Assignments and activities that are given in school are designed to help you prepare for life after school even if the work is not always exciting. *Work projects* teach you how to organize and get your ideas on paper. *Presenting* in front of your class helps build confidence when you communicate. *Sports*, of course, teach you about teamwork, leadership, and skill development. And bad work habits can teach you about struggling and how to avoid working harder not smarter.

Struggles are real in school. Even with all my honor roll certificates, the transition to high school was difficult for me, and I struggled early. I was lazy, and my priorities were out of alignment. The material was also hard for me to understand. At the advice of my counselor, I sought out tutoring. I started participating more in class by asking questions when I didn't understand the material. When I reset my priorities and asked for

Some people see asking for help as a sign of weakness, and by admitting they need help, they in turn feel like a failure.

help, my grades slowly improved. For some people it is hard to ask for help. Some people see asking for help as a sign of weakness, and by admitting they need help, they in turn feel like a failure. Asking for help when you need it is a smart choice, not a weak one. Don't be afraid to ask!

Better Choices. Better Habits.

Success in the classroom and in school is a choice. Choose better habits. My goal in school was simple—get straight A's. After creating the goal of what I wanted to accomplish, I set a priority list. My priority list looked like this:

Homework
Studying
Gym
Friends

Create better habits by having someone hold you accountable, such as a study partner or accountability coach. A good partner is NOT your best friend. A good study partner or accountability coach is someone who will help you focus and not deter you from the work. A good habit to practice is turning off your cell phone, occasionally, to get rid of distractions. And yes, that includes turning off Twitter, Facebook, and Instagram. Turning off your phone every once in a while is a good habit to adopt. It is a temporary one because our phones can be useful. A smartphone is useful when prioritizing tasks. Smartphones are equipped with calendars, alarms, and notifications that act as reminders. Reminders help busy people stay on top of things. With a busy schedule, tasks can get brushed off or forgotten, but setting reminders will help. The cause of my struggles in school was poor planning. I chose better habits, and as a result, I'm still ballin!

Full-Court Pressure

In basketball, a full-court press is when the defense applies pressure to the offensive team the entire length of the court before the inbound pass and after the inbound pass. This defensive style is common in basketball and effective at getting the offensive team rattled. The pressure is aggressive and continuous. There

Peer pressure is being constantly bombarded by your peers to do something that most of the time goes against your morals and values.

is a full-court press happening to young adults—peer pressure. Peer pressure exists and is toxic for young adults and emerging leaders. There is a need to fit in and be liked by your peers. Peer pressure is being constantly bombarded by your peers to do something that most of the time goes against your morals and values.

Peer pressure can be avoided if you first surround yourself with a positive group of peers and secondly learn to say and be ok with NO. If you are experiencing peer pressure, remember you have a choice. In the next chapter, you will learn that a *no* is ok and a necessary response in certain situations. Just say no! As cliché as that sounds, that's how simple it is. A simple no could be the difference between you leading a life on your terms or someone else's terms. As a student-athlete, I was always a target. I have been offered to smoke and drink on numerous occasions, but I turned it down because I understood the bigger picture—living life on my terms not someone else's. It is important you understand that you have a choice.

Not all peer pressure, like not all losses, is detrimental. A pressure or push to excel is a constant thought on my mind. I put most of that pressure on myself, but I also hear it from my classmates before a big game when they ask things like, *"How much you dropping tonight?"* or *"I'm expecting big things out of you, man."* That pressure to excel creates a fear of failing. In those instances, I fear

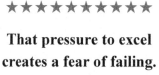

That pressure to excel creates a fear of failing.

failing because I don't want to disappoint others or fail to meet their expectations. Sound familiar? What matters most is that you gave 100 percent effort and 100 percent attitude.

Leading In and Out of the Game

My mother always told me to be a "leader and not a follower, to make my own choices, and to stand out from the crowd." Leadership to me is a person running things and in control. A leader is a person of integrity that is true to themselfs and inspires others to be great. Leading can look like the captain of the team, a project leader, a club president, a store manager, or a big brother. Taking on a leadership role early will teach you about a higher level of responsibility and how to give and receive feedback. You will disprove the naysayers that believe young people make poor leaders if you step up, emerge from the bench, and take your place in and out of the game.

How To Lead—Three-Point Play to Leadership

If you are considering taking on a leadership role and are unsure about how to lead, there are three rules you should follow as a first step to help build your confidence to lead: *Learn. Ask. Be an example*.

1) *Learn* about what it is that you are going to be leading. Make sure you have acquired as much possible knowledge about the subject or sport or workplace that you will be leading.

2) *Asking* is not a sign of weakness. Don't be afraid to ask for advice about anything. Ask a mentor or trusted advisor. In chapter five, you learned that mentors are great resources for young adults and emerging leaders throughout life and career. Asking is not following. Asking doesn't mean you are incapable of leading. Asking means you are getting knowledge that you don't have from a knowledgeable and more experienced person and using that information to help you lead more effectively.

3) *Be an example* that people want to aspire to. Lead with your actions. If people see you working hard and getting results, they too will want to do better. Lead with your words. Be mindful of the promises you make. If you make a promise, keep it. In life, your word is EVERYTHING! If you break a promise, you lose a person's trust. Lead with a strong set of values. Work ethic is your

★ ★ ★ ★ ★ ★ ★ ★ ★ ★

Be an example that people aspire to.

★ ★ ★ ★ ★ ★ ★ ★ ★ ★

85

work-related values. Core values are the principles you live by, through and through. They are uncompromising and non-negotiable.

Values: Keeping It 100

Core values are important to me because they keep me humble and true to myself. Creating values as a young adult will help you find out more about who you are and what truly matters to you. At age sixteen, you have a set of values that show up when you make tough decisions or are faced with peer pressure. Those values, however, may change when you reach eighteen or twenty-three. By establishing values early in life, you become more centered, you become less tempted by peer pressure, and you begin to develop a strong belief system. Values, in my opinion, are those things that you will do anything to protect.

Throughout all of your existing and future success, you must stay true to yourself and your beliefs. My core values are *faith, family, friends*. *Faith* is my anchor. Being raised in a Christian household, I have always been taught to put Jesus first. This has kept me grounded. Faith is vital to my life and a core value that is unchanging. *Family* is everything. Where would I be without the support and unconditional love of my family? Family is the one constant in an ever-changing world. *Friendships* are important to me, just as important as family. I value the people that have always been there supporting me and "keeping it 100" – being honest and truthful . I need people around me to keep it 100 and keep me humble.

Overtime—A Little Something Extra

My high school basketball team went on a losing streak right before we had to get ready for a league that was the toughest in our state. Through these tough times, it feels as if nothing is going right and that nothing will ever go right. However, using your failures as motivation to improve is vital for a successful life. Losses show you what you need to learn and what you need to improve. We were able to get our heads on straight, take all the positives from our losses, grow on them, take the negatives, and learn from them. We finished the pre-league games 2-1 against some good teams. This is a prime example of using failure as motivation and looking at its upside instead of its downside.

Now Do This!

★ ★ ★ ★ ★ ★ ★ ★ ★ ★

Scan the box below or type the URL into your browser and watch a short video of Tiana speaking on this topic. Select the video

"Leadership and Influence"

https://www.youtube.com/tianaempowers

★ ★ ★ ★ ★ ★ ★ ★ ★ ★

Chapter 8

Bad Words. Good Advice.

"To change ourselves effectively, we first had to change our perceptions."
—**Stephen R. Covey**

We give words power. A dictionary is filled with words and definitions that describe their meaning and intent. Words often have more than one meaning when used in a different context. Words can be hurtful and discouraging, but they can also be uplifting and empowering. It's not the person uttering the words that gives them power but the person on the receiving end. "Sticks and stones will break my bones, but words will never hurt me." If you believe that statement, then you understand how to diffuse the power of words. However, you are an exception and among an exclusive group of individuals with high self-esteem and thick skin. What about the rest of us? And yes I said *us* because there are times that I too struggle with this. So, how do we take these bad words and use them to our advantage? Well, for starters, we redefine them. We give them new meaning. We need to eliminate some words and redefine others.

Think of it this way: remove and repurpose. *Removing* certain words from our vocabulary is a big step toward reconditioning our thoughts and action. A word like "should" is a form of procrastination and yields no fruit for success-creators and forward-thinkers. *Repurpose* means to use or convert something into another format, to change something so that it can be used for a different purpose. *Failure* is a word we can repurpose by changing its meaning from bad to good. Let's flip more words and make them work for us.

Bad word: **Adversity** is an extremely unfavorable experience or hardship.

Good advice: A hardship can produce humility. Sometimes it takes an unpleasant experience for us to realize how truly blessed we were. That type of misfortune makes us more appreciative and grateful.

Bad word: **Blind spots** are obstructions that impede our view and stop us from taking action.

Good advice: Blind spots prevent you from seeing the full scope of the situation. Hesitation, maybes, and a lack of risk-taking could all be indications of a blind spot.

Bad word: **Desperation** is defined as hopelessness and extreme anxiety.

Good advice: Desperation creates urgency. When something is urgent, it's usually important and that helps to eliminate procrastination.

Bad word: **Discomfort** is a state of feeling awkward, uneasy, or embarrassed.

Good advice: Comfort can breed laziness. Laziness is the antithesis of effort. Discomfort keeps you sharp, alert, and humble.

Bad word: **Disruptions** interrupt the order of things.

Good advice: Disruptions reveal your level of comfort and challenge you to be flexible.

Bad word: **Failure** is not achieving that which you set out to achieve.

Good advice: Failure is information. It guides, teaches, and motivates you to do better. Failures give you an opportunity for a do-over and point you in a new and often better direction.

Bad word: **Fear** is apprehension caused by the anticipation of danger.

Good advice: Fear is an indication that you need to "proceed with caution." Fear provides insight into a situation to help you make an informed decision.

Bad word: **Limit** is the furthest point you can go, measured by a minimum and a maximum that is allowed.

Good advice: There is no limit to your success! Remove "limit" from your vocabulary and replace it with possibility. Where there are limits, there are restrictions. Strive for uninhibited, overflowing, expansive, and tremendously massive success!!

Bad word: **Losses** are defined as no longer having something.

Good advice   Losses can be a blessing if the loss caused you harm and interfered with your values. Measure the loss by the gain that comes after. If what you lost was toxic, causing distress, and holding you back, then the loss was worth taking.

Bad word: **Maybe** is an indifferent attitude or response, neither a yes nor a no, and causes indecisiveness.

Good advice: Maybe is a gray area without definitiveness, a copout word when your gut reaction is clear. Remove maybes and be decisive. Do you think leaders can get away with a maybe? A no or yes is really okay.

Bad word: **Mistakes** are errors or an unwise decision caused by poor judgement.

Good advice: Mistakes point out our flaws and serve as a reminder that we are human.

Bad word: **No** is to disagree or refuse when asked. It's a firm remark without any gray area.

Good advice: No is an indication perhaps that something is not right. Is there an indication that this is not the right move? A no can be a refreshing response for the sender not necessarily the receiver. Professionally and tactfully done, a no can prevent others from taking advantage of you. It's a confidence-boosting move.

Bad word: **Normal** is the usual standard, ordinary, typical, common.

Good advice: Who wants to be normal? This is not a word that you would consider bad at first glance—until you compare normal to exceptional. Normal or usual is the antithesis of extraordinary. Who wants to blend in when you can blend out? Embrace different ideas and unconventional processes. Don't put yourself in a box with conformists and followers. Lead differently by being different.

Bad word: **Pain** is a feeling of discomfort.

Good advice: Pain is an agonizing reminder of our discomfort. Discomfort is a part of our growth. No pain, no gain, no growth.

Bad word: **Problem** is a difficult situation.

Good advice: When we see a problem, our gut reaction is to run away. Before you run, analyze the problem. Look at it from different angles. If the right decision is to run, then run. But don't default to running away if you need to run toward the problem instead. Repurpose the word "problem" and see it as opportunity to practice problem-solving and critical-thinking skills.

Bad word: **Quit** is to give up, to stop.

Good advice: When you feel like quitting, be reminded of this quote, *"This too shall pass."* Whether the reasons are monumental or minute, quitting is not a viable option if you want results.

Bad word: **Rejection** is when you are on the receiving end of a no.

Good advice: This is an opportunity to ask questions. *Reflect*, use hindsight, and think about what you could do differently next time. *Correct* and revise your approach or strategy. *Project* and propel yourself forward, leveraging the rejection as another chance to do better.

Bad word: **Risk** is the chance or possibility of something going wrong.

Good advice: Don't avoid risks; take calculated ones. A calculated risk is a carefully thought out risk, taking all possibilities into account, and deducing the best course of action. Is it low-risk, moderate-risk, or high-risk? What is the likelihood that something could go wrong? What is my conclusion based on? Taking calculated risks requires analytical and critical thinking. If you play it safe all the time, you'll never reach your full potential.

Bad word: **Should** in this definition is accompanied by "have," which is a form of regret.

Good advice: A "should have" is a form of regret or guilt about taking action or a lack of taking action. Reflect on your decision and learn from it, but then move forward. Don't "should" on yourself.

Bad word:	**Shut Up**, an unpleasant phrase that means to keep quiet.
Good advice:	The best advice I received was from a millionaire: *"In business and in life, you need to know when to suit up, show up, and shut up!"* Period.

Bad word:	**Try** is an attempt made at something, as in *"I will try to do better."*
Good advice:	Don't try. DO! Don't try to do better—do better. Don't try to be kind—be kind. *Try* can be a bad word when used in that context. Avoid using "try" and say "I will." I will DO my best, not I will *try* to do my best.

We give words power or render them powerless. There are words that need to be *removed* from your vocabulary because they breed negativity and cause delay. Some words can be *repurposed* by redefining the word and giving it a new meaning that we can use for good.

Now Do This!

★★★★★★★★★★

Scan the box below or type the URL into your browser and watch a short video on this topic. Select the video

"Don't SHOULD on Yourself. #1 Best Advice"

https://www.youtube.com/tianaempowers

★★★★★★★★★★

Conclusion

"Success is stumbling from failure to failure with no loss of enthusiasm."
—Winston Churchill

When my eldest son was about five years old, he took swimming lessons from our local YMCA. It was important he learned how to swim at an early age. Swimming was a necessity, especially if you lived in the beautiful and always sunny California. Swimming was also an important survival lesson. As the parent of a toddler, my goal was to protect him and to teach him how to respect the water and not fear it.

As soon as he started swimming lessons, he loved it. He immediately took to the water. I watched as he and the instructor bounced around in the water, she holding him as she walked the length of the shallow pool. I watched as he learned to kick holding onto the side of the pool, arms stretched and legs pumping at full speed, making big splashes in the water. I watched as he would swim from the instructor to the side of the pool and back, tiny arms and tiny legs moving in sync. He was swimming! He learned how to swim and had enjoyed the learning process.

One Saturday afternoon I was unable to take my son to swimming lessons, and my mother graciously accepted the task. While I was out of town, I received a disturbing call from my mother. She said that my son almost drowned while taking his lessons. His usual instructor was not there, and they replaced her with another instructor. The instructor took his group to the deep end of the pool, something his usual teacher had not done. The bigger pool was longer and deeper—much, much deeper. This instructor did not assess his skill level before placing him in the bigger pool. He started swimming the length of the pool, using a kickboard as his guide and security. He reached about halfway and somehow the board escaped from his hands, and he went underwater. His head popped up, arms flailing, as he looked for something to hold onto. He tried to swim and went under the water a second time. He managed to get his head above water again, but by the third time, his head went under and didn't come back up. My mother appeared to be the only one who noticed my son struggling. Both the lifeguard and the instructor in that area did not notice what was happening until my mother was making a beeline toward the pool. She reached in to pull him up but, unable to swim herself, she could not reach him. Other parents who saw this taking place yelled for help. It was then a lifeguard on the other side of the pool, not in that area, who jumped in, and they both emerged from the water, my son gasping for air.

From then on out my son did not want to get into another pool. He was apprehensive and rightfully so after his experience. I would try to ease him back into the water, but he was combative and scared. He was afraid of experiencing that horrific event again. Sometimes we feel like that when we experience rejection, a setback, an occasional misstep or tumble, a mistake, or an epic failure. The failure makes us feel like we are drowning, unable to pull ourselves up. The failure creates a fear within us so great that we choose not to take risks. We become doubtful and uncertain of our capabilities. We allow the experience to defeat us. Remember, these unpleasant experiences teach us. They teach us critical thinking, creative problem-solving skills, effort (work required), and attitude (motivation). The failure *opens up a new pathway of unexplored strength and resolve, which would have not otherwise been realized had we not experienced the failure in the first place.*

Today, my son is seventeen years old and an outstanding swimmer. He's a fish in the water: backflips, front flips, and handstands. He made a choice. It's the same choice you have. Will I allow this experience to stop me from reaching my full potential? Will I give up and give in to defeat? Will I unleash my inner champion and address my fears head on? Am I going to be satisfied with ordinary, or do I want to be extraordinary? Malala didn't give up pursuing her dream of education for young women after being shot in the head. She got bolder and continues to do remarkable work. Diana Nyad didn't retreat and retire her bathing suit after four failed attempts. She *failed forward* into a spectacular victory.

So let me remind you of the misconception of failure. It is NOT bad and fatal to your career, life, and relationships. Failure, as you have read in this book, does open up a new pathway of unexplored strength and resolve. Would we have realized that strength if we had not experienced the failure in the first place? This type of thinking is a paradigm shift and a new way of thinking. It goes against what we are taught in our culture, which is why some of you will embrace this idea and some of you won't. That's the hard truth.

Are you a success-creator or a doubt-creator? Are you an educator with an open mind? Are you an organization that believes that there are other ways to correct behavior and performance that do not rely solely on penalties and punishment? Are you a person who believes there is no limit to your success? I know my answer— what's yours? Don't tell me. Show me!

References

Biography.com Editors. "Steven Spielberg Biography." The Biography.com website, A&E Networks. Retrieved on January 13, 2016. http://www.biography.com/people/steven-spielberg-9490621.

Krakovsky, Marina. March/April 2007. "The Effort Effect." *Stanford Alumni Magazine*. Retrieved on January 15, 2016. https://alumni.stanford.edu/get/page/magazine/article/?article_id=32124.

McClintock, Pamela. May 7, 2013. "Box Office Milestone: 'Iron Man 3' Hits $1 Billion Worldwide." *Hollywood Reporter*. Retrieved on December 15, 2015. http://www.hollywoodreporter.com/news/box-office-milestone-iron-man-524587

Nyad, Diana. Filmed December 2013. "Never, ever give up." *TEDWoman 2013*. Retrieved on December 12, 2015. http://www.ted.com/talks/diana_nyad_never_ever_give_up.

Rideout, Vicky. "Common Sense Census: Media Used by Tweens and Teens." Common Sense Media. Retrieved on January 13, 2016. http://www.commonsensemedia.org/census.

U.S. Department of Education. "Competency-Based Learning or Personalized Learning." Retrieved on January 13, 2016. http://www.ed.gov/oii-news/competency-based-learning-or-personalized-learning

Yousafzai, Malala. "Malala's Story." Retrieved on December 15, 2015. https://www.malala.org/malalas-story.

Acknowledgments

First and foremost, I'd like to thank God for bestowing upon me the gift of inspiring people with my words and life experiences. I want to thank my husband and business partner Will Alexander for your enormous support and patience. Your contribution to this book does not go unnoticed. I appreciate your wise counsel, even at times when I didn't want to hear it. You told me, in a loving way, what I needed to hear, not what I wanted to hear. You are my trusted advisor, my advocate, and my best friend. I love you unconditionally.

I want to thank my two boys, Tian and Salim. Tian, you have emerged as a young leader over the past four years. Your contribution to this book is an incredible achievement. Relish and celebrate this accomplishment and never put limitations on achieving success. Salim, thank you for letting Mommy work and write. It was challenging at times, but you kept me entertained … most of the time.

A BIG thank you to my marketing and video production team at Epiphany Marketing. Rasheed, you interpreted my vision and designed a stellar cover. I appreciate your dedication to my "passion project" and your support of my vision as well as my book.

Many thanks to Cliff and his team at eFluential Publishing. The timing of us working together could not have been better.

Thank you Krystal Miguel for your continued support and for utilizing *Undefeatable* as a learning tool to encourage your students. You are lifting up the future leaders of our generation one by one.

Thanks Steve Lerer and the faculty at UC Merced for opening your doors and inviting me to impart wisdom to the students. I am officially an "Honorary Bobcat."

Thank you to every person who has attended my workshops and training sessions over the years. I am especially grateful to the organizations that have placed their people in my care for mentorship, coaching, and training.

Thank you Rick Hodge and Los Angeles Southwest College for educating me about the challenges facing young adults and emerging leaders as they prepare for a career after college.

A special thanks to my Ambassadors—my family and friends that proclaim their support by posting, tweeting, blogging, and spreading the word about the book. I am humbled by your generosity and grateful for your love and friendship.

And thank you to every person who reads this book and walks away with a better outlook. You are not your failures!

More About the Author

As owner of an organizational training and development practice, **Tiana** has provided training and development workshops to hundreds of professionals throughout the United States. She is the voice for modern-day professionals, working in tandem with colleges and employers to foster a more confident and competent workforce in the new economy.

Her passion for raising the bar in talent development was spawned through years in management and honed during an impressive and longstanding career in the retail, food and beverage, and financial industries. At age seventeen, she was one of the youngest managers overseeing day-to-day business operations, directing employee development, and leading the acquisition of talent. A pivotal moment in her career is when she was appointed by a CEO to the strategic planning team, sparking her interest in organizational culture and establishing her as a skilled speaker. Her greatest achievement was nurturing her employees' potential and moving them forward up the career ladder.

In 2011 Tiana launched **Tiana Sanchez Professional Coaching Services**, an organizational training and development practice that is committed to helping individuals build up key competencies that help them perform better in their careers. Through trainer-led workshops and competency-based learning, she helps managers, emerging leaders, and students RE-THINK their leadership potential and RE-DEFINE success.

Tiana has coached, trained, and developed the top talent for some well-known organizations such as Southern California Edison, Hot

Dog on a Stick, Sugar Foods, L'Oréal, Verizon, and Time Warner Cable Arena.

Tiana is a sought-after speaker and has delivered poignant workshops for educational institutions including UC Merced, Los Angeles Southwest College, University of La Verne, and California State University San Bernardino. She is a two-time published author, spreading the idea that "failures are necessary and make us great" and readying herself for the TED Talk stage.

The *Undefeatable* book has been featured in the media with speaker and philanthropist Melanie Mack of Black Hollywood Live Phenomenal Women and Myles of Success WHP 580 News Radio. Tiana enjoys a vegan lifestyle, kickboxing, spinning and resides in Southern California with her husband and two kids.

Bite-Size Curriculum

60-Minute Lessons for the
Progressive Learner

Lesson 1 – The UPside of Failure

Curriculum Designed for Educators, Trainers, Young Adults

Lesson 1 – The UPside of Failure

Tips for Use

Curriculum may be used as a tool for professional coaching, peer-to-peer coaching, guidance counseling, and career counseling.

Overview

The UPside to Failure lesson introduces participants to failure as an experience we all face and the benefits of that experience. Failure opens up a new pathway of unexplored strength and resolve which would have not otherwise been realized had we not experienced the failure in the first place. Video links are provided at the end of each chapter to build on what was read in the book. Use links as needed.

Objective

Targeting young adults and emerging leaders, the objective is to start a dialogue about the benefits of experiencing failure. Failure is information that can be used to develop critical thinking skills, problem solving skills, and spark new ideas.

You Will Need

- ✓ A group leader or facilitator
- ✓ Flip chart or white board
- ✓ Copies of the book, *F'd UP*
- ✓ Notebook or journal
- ✓ Feedback form
- ✓ Markers

Lesson 1 – The UPside of Failure

Curriculum Designed for Educators, Trainers, Young Adults

Lesson 1 – The UPside of Failure

Before Lesson

Writing Activity: (5-10 min)

1. Ask participants to describe a time they failed at something—an experience when they did not perform up to an expectation. Was it playing a sport? Playing an instrument?
2. Ask them to describe what happened and how it made them feel. What did they say to themselves? What did they hear others say?

After Lesson (5-10 min)

1. Ask participants to complete the ten-question feedback form accessible in this book and at www.nolimit2your success.com/forms.
2. Discuss questions as a group. Listen. Ask more questions.
3. Encourage participants to reflect, write, and share.

Small Group Activity – Resiliency (20 min)

Break into small groups of four to five people. Ask participants to think of a time, possibly as a child, where they were less concerned about making a mistake, a time when their confidence was shaken but not overcome by defeat. Ask each person to describe the situation and then discuss the "why." Examples: learning to walk, ride a bike, skate, play an instrument, play a sport.

Large Group Discussion – Society Reimagined (20 min)

As a large group discussion, talk about different ways people view failures in our society. Ask them to imagine a society where failure is viewed as information to solve problems that enhance learning and development. What would that look like in school? At work? In social settings? In life?

Feedback Form

Lesson (circle) 1 2 3 4 5 6 7 8

Respond to the questions honestly after reading the assigned chapter in the book *F'd UP: The UPside of Failure*.

1. Did you find the subject matter in this chapter informative and helpful? Why or why not?

2. What was a new concept or idea you learned in this chapter?

3. How did this chapter help you to deal with failures differently?

4. How did the information in this chapter help change your perspective on failure?

5. After reading this chapter, what do you need to STOP doing?

6. After reading this chapter, what do you need to START doing?

7. After reading this chapter, what do you need to CONTINUE doing?

8. What was your biggest takeaway from the chapter?

9. Who would you recommend read this chapter? Be specific.

10. Will you apply what you have learned? Why or why not? How?

Notes Lesson 1 – The UPside of Failure

Lesson 2 – Failure Is the New Success

Curriculum Designed for Educators, Trainers, Students

Lesson 2 – Failure Is the New Success

Tips for Use

Curriculum may be used as a tool for professional coaching, peer-to-peer coaching, guidance counseling, and career counseling.

Overview

Failure Is the New Success lesson teaches participants about perspective. Learning from failures and applying what we learn becomes part of the success-attaining process. Failure is matter of perspective, and individuals that have a fixed mindset believe success is achieved as a result of innate abilities. Video links are provided at the end of each chapter to build on what was read in the book. Use links as needed.

Objective

Targeting young adults and emerging leaders, the objective is to start a dialogue about changing their outlook on failure. By developing a "growth mindset," individuals thrive on challenges and see failure as a springboard for growth.

You Will Need
- ✓ A group leader or facilitator
- ✓ Flip chart or white board
- ✓ Copies of the book, *F'd UP*
- ✓ Notebook or journal
- ✓ Screen/monitor
- ✓ Feedback form
- ✓ Markers

Lesson 2 – Failure Is the New Success

Curriculum Designed for Educators, Trainers, Students

Lesson 2 – Failure Is the New Success

Before Lesson

Writing Activity: (5-10 min)

1. Ask students to define success. What words come to mind? Ask participants to write five to ten words that represent success as they understand it today.

2. Ask participants to draw a picture illustrating the path of success. The path or road map must include a start and a destination.

After Lesson (5-10 min)

1. Ask participants to complete the ten-question feedback form accessible in this book and at www.nolimit2your success.com/forms.

2. Discuss questions as a group. Listen. Ask more questions.

3. Encourage participants to reflect, write, and share.

Small Group Activity – Perspective (20 min)

Break into small groups of four to five people. Ask each participant to think of a recent failure and answer the following questions: What other information can I gather from this situation? Is there another way to view this problem, issue, or situation? What positive aspects can I pull out of this experience? Who else can I ask for objective feedback? Write. Share in small groups.

Large Group Discussion – Never Give UP (20 min)

Watch the Diana Nyad TEDWomen 2013 talk and have a discussion about what it means to "never give up." View the video at https://www.ted.com/talks/diana_nyad_never_ever_give_up.

Feedback Form

Lesson (circle) 1 2 3 4 5 6 7 8

Respond to the questions honestly after reading the assigned chapter in the book *F'd UP: The UPside of Failure.*

1. Did you find the subject matter in this chapter informative and helpful? Why or why not?

2. What was a new concept or idea you learned in this chapter?

3. How did this chapter help you to deal with failures differently?

4. How did the information in this chapter help change your perspective on failure?

5. After reading this chapter, what do you need to STOP doing?

6. After reading this chapter, what do you need to START doing?

7. After reading this chapter, what do you need to CONTINUE doing?

8. What was your biggest takeaway from the chapter?

9. Who would you recommend read this chapter? Be specific.

10. Will you apply what you have learned? Why or why not? How?

Notes Lesson 2 – Failure Is the New Success

Lesson 3 – Don't Quit. Get Bold.

Curriculum Designed for Educators, Trainers, Students

Lesson 3 – Don't Quit. Get Bold.

Tips for Use
Curriculum may be used as a tool for professional coaching, peer-to-peer coaching, guidance counseling, and career counseling.

Overview
The Don't Quit Get Bold lesson introduces participants to boldness and radical change and why daring to be different, and doing it unapologetically, is a defeat killer. Participants learn how to stand out, live audaciously, and make an impact. Video links are provided at the end of each chapter to build on what was read in the book. Use links as needed.

Objective
Targeting young adults and emerging leaders, the objective is to teach students to forget popularity and think unpopular. Blend out, don't blend in with everyone and be ordinary. Who wants to be ordinary when you can be extraordinary?

You Will Need
- ✓ A group leader or facilitator
- ✓ Flip chart or white board
- ✓ Copies of the book, *F'd UP*
- ✓ Notebook or journal
- ✓ Feedback form
- ✓ Markers

Lesson 3 – Don't Quit. Get Bold.

Curriculum Designed for Educators, Trainers, Students

Lesson 3 – Don't Quit. Get Bold.

Before Lesson

Writing Activity: (5-10 min)

1. Ask participants to write about a time they quit or gave up something. Ask them to share the reasons why they quit. Did they give up because they were afraid to fail? Explore reasons.

2. Ask participants what they could accomplish today if they were not afraid of failing or not meeting an expectation?

After Lesson (5-10 min)

1. Ask participants to complete the ten-question feedback form accessible in this book and at www.nolimit2your success.com/forms.

2. Discuss questions as a group. Listen. Ask more questions.

3. Encourage participants to reflect, write, and share.

Small Group Activity –Boldness (20 min)

Break into groups of four to five people. Ask the group to discuss what it means to be bold. Ask participants to identify a celebrity, public figure, or someone they know that embodies boldness. What are their characteristics? Define and list responses. Ask participants to circle traits that they aspire to have.

Large Group Discussion – Boldness II (20 min)

Read Malala's story in chapter three and answer the questions in the chapter. Discuss responses as a group.

Feedback Form

Lesson (circle) 1 2 3 4 5 6 7 8

Respond to the questions honestly after reading the assigned chapter in the book *F'd UP: The UPside of Failure*.

1. Did you find the subject matter in this chapter informative and helpful? Why or why not?

2. What was a new concept or idea you learned in this chapter?

3. How did this chapter help you to deal with failures differently?

4. How did the information in this chapter help change your perspective on failure?

5. After reading this chapter, what do you need to STOP doing?

6. After reading this chapter, what do you need to START doing?

7. After reading this chapter, what do you need to CONTINUE doing?

8. What was your biggest takeaway from the chapter?

9. Who would you recommend read this chapter? Be specific.

10. Will you apply what you have learned? Why or why not? How?

Notes Lesson 3 – Don't Quit. Get Bold.

Lesson 4 – Failures Make Us Great

Curriculum Designed for Educators, Trainers, Students

Lesson 4 – Failures Make Us Great

Tips for Use
Curriculum may be used as a tool for professional coaching, peer-to-peer coaching, guidance counseling, and career counseling.

Overview
The Failures Make Us Great lesson challenges each participant to redefine success and find the "upside" in their own experiences. Most people only see the "after" of a person's success and not the "before." What does the before look like? Video links are provided at the end of each chapter to build on what was read in the book. Use links as needed.

Objective
Targeting young adults and emerging leaders, the objective is to help them understand their feelings and thoughts about experiencing failure.

You Will Need
- ✓ A group leader or facilitator
- ✓ Flip chart or white board
- ✓ Copies of the book, *F'd UP*
- ✓ Notebook or journal
- ✓ Feedback form
- ✓ Markers

Lesson 4 – Failures Make Us Great

Curriculum Designed for Educators, Trainers, Students

Lesson 4 – Failures Make Us Great

Before Lesson

Writing Activity: (5-10 min)

1. Ask participants to write about an enjoyable experience, a time when they excelled at something.
2. What did they accomplish that was great and worth recognition? What made the accomplishment great? Explain.

After Lesson (5-10 min)

1. Ask participants to complete the ten-question feedback form accessible in this book and at www.nolimit2your success.com/forms.
2. Discuss questions as a group. Listen. Ask more questions.
3. Encourage participants to reflect, write, and share.

Small Group Activity – When I fail... (20 min)

Break into small groups of four to five people. Appoint a scribe for the group. Ask each person to complete the sentence: "When I experience failures, I have a tendency to..." Discuss similarities and differences within the group. Share the top ten common responses in the large group discussion. Ask the scribe of the group to write the top ten on a flip chart and post it around the room.

Large Group Discussion (20 min)

The facilitator will review the responses as a large group discussion, pointing out similarities and differences. Note positive responses and negative responses. Expound on the responses.

Feedback Form

Lesson (circle) 1   2   3   4   5   6   7   8

Respond to the questions honestly after reading the assigned chapter in the book *F'd UP: The UPside of Failure.*

1. Did you find the subject matter in this chapter informative and helpful? Why or why not?

2. What was a new concept or idea you learned in this chapter?

3. How did this chapter help you to deal with failures differently?

4. How did the information in this chapter help change your perspective on failure?

5. After reading this chapter, what do you need to STOP doing?

6. After reading this chapter, what do you need to START doing?

7. After reading this chapter, what do you need to CONTINUE doing?

8. What was your biggest takeaway from the chapter?

9. Who would you recommend read this chapter? Be specific.

10. Will you apply what you have learned? Why or why not? How?

Notes Lesson 4 – Failures Make Us Great

_____

_____

_____

_____

_____

_____

_____

_____

_____

_____

_____

_____

_____

_____

_____

_____

_____

_____

_____

_____

_____

Lesson 5 – The UPside of Change

Curriculum Designed for Educators, Trainers, Students

Lesson 5 – The UPside of Change

Tips for Use

Curriculum may be used as a tool for professional coaching, peer-to-peer coaching, guidance counseling, and career counseling. Designed for high school and college students.

Overview

The UPside to Change lesson introduces participants to change and how it causes a necessary disruption to our life, particularly in how young adults approach their careers. Change is unavoidable, and it causes us to rethink our motives, rethink our plans, and rethink our potential. Video links are provided at the end of each chapter to build on what was read in the book. Use links as needed.

Objective

Targeting young adults and emerging leaders, the objective is to change the way young adults think about life and career. Provide young adults and emerging leaders with a new approach and resources: mentorship, internships, work-based learning, and competency-based education.

You Will Need
- ✓ A group leader or facilitator
- ✓ Flip chart or white board
- ✓ Copies of the book, *F'd UP*
- ✓ Notebook or journal
- ✓ Feedback form
- ✓ Markers

Lesson 5 – The UPside of Change

Curriculum Designed for Educators, Trainers, Students

Lesson 5 – The UPside of Change

Before Lesson

Writing Activity: (5-10 min)

1. Ask participants to write a list of things they want to accomplish in life, career, school, etc. Have them prioritize the list from one to ten.
2. Ask participants to write one to three obstacles that could cause a setback and disrupt their plans.

After Lesson (5-10 min)

1. Ask participants to complete the ten-question feedback form accessible in this book and at www.nolimit2your success.com/forms.
2. Discuss questions as a group. Listen. Ask more questions.
3. Encourage participants to reflect, write, and share.

Small Group Activity – Peer to Peer Mentorship (20 min)

Ask each participant to partner up. You may assign partners at random. Ask each participant to think of a problem they are facing. Participants take turns mentoring each other in an area where they are seeking advice. Avoid highly sensitive topics.

Large Group Discussion – Change (20 min)

As a large group, ask, "What makes change so difficult for us to accept? Why is change easier to accept when we know the benefits?" Make a connection between change and skill development.

Feedback Form

Lesson (circle) 1 2 3 4 5 6 7 8

Respond to the questions honestly after reading the assigned chapter in the book *F'd UP: The UPside of Failure*.

1. Did you find the subject matter in this chapter informative and helpful? Why or why not?

2. What was a new concept or idea you learned in this chapter?

3. How did this chapter help you to deal with failures differently?

4. How did the information in this chapter help change your perspective on failure?

5. After reading this chapter, what do you need to STOP doing?

6. After reading this chapter, what do you need to START doing?

7. After reading this chapter, what do you need to CONTINUE doing?

8. What was your biggest takeaway from the chapter?

9. Who would you recommend read this chapter? Be specific.

10. Will you apply what you have learned? Why or why not? How?

Notes Lesson 5 – The UPside of Change

_____

_____

_____

_____

_____

_____

_____

_____

_____

_____

_____

_____

_____

_____

_____

_____

_____

_____

_____

_____

_____

_____

_____

Lesson 6 – Unleashing Your Inner Champion

Curriculum Designed for Educators, Trainers, Students

Lesson 6 – Unleashing Your Inner Champion

Tips for Use

Curriculum may be used as a tool for professional coaching, peer-to-peer coaching, guidance counseling, and career counseling.

Overview

The Unleashing Your Inner Champion lesson introduces participants to the meaning of discomfort and the importance of confronting fears. It teaches them that sometimes you will have to "sit in your discomfort" and endure a certain level of pain and discomfort to obtain a greater reward. Video links are provided at the end of each chapter to build on what was read in the book. Use links as needed.

Objective

Targeting young adults and emerging leaders, the objective is to teach participants to identify and confront fears and get comfortable with being uncomfortable. Enduring a level of discomfort can create a sense of urgency and push people toward action.

You Will Need

✓ A group leader or facilitator
✓ Flip chart or white board
✓ Copies of the book, *F'd UP*
✓ Notebook or journal
✓ Post-its and blank paper
✓ Feedback form
✓ Markers

Lesson 6 – Unleashing Your Inner Champion

Curriculum Designed for Educators, Trainers, Students

Lesson 6 – Unleashing Your Inner Champion

Before Lesson
Writing Activity: (5-10 min)

1. Ask participants to respond to this question: *Are you confident? Why or why not? What activities increase your confidence?* Ask participants to include talent, skills, expertise.

2. Now ask participants to respond to this question: *What activity or activities decrease your confidence?*

After Lesson (5-10 min)

1. Ask participants to complete the ten-question feedback form accessible in this book and at www.nolimit2your success.com/forms.

2. Discuss questions as a group. Listen. Ask more questions.

3. Encourage participants to reflect, write, and share.

Individual Activity – Win/Lose/Fail (20 min)
Draw a box. Draw two lines so that there are three columns. In the first column, write the word *failure* at the very top. In the second column, write the word *losses*. In the third column, write the word *wins*. Think of a situation for each category. Answer the questions: What did it look like? What did it sound like? How did it make me feel?

Large Group Discussion (20 min)

Write columns on flip chart or white board. Ask each participant to write responses to each question and for all three categories on a Post-it. Place the Post-its in the appropriate category on the board or flip chart. Discuss findings as a group.

Feedback Form

Lesson (circle)   1   2   3   4   5   6   7   8

Respond to the questions honestly after reading the assigned chapter in the book *F'd UP: The UPside of Failure*.

1. Did you find the subject matter in this chapter informative and helpful? Why or why not?

2. What was a new concept or idea you learned in this chapter?

3. How did this chapter help you to deal with failures differently?

4. How did the information in this chapter help change your perspective on failure?

5. After reading this chapter, what do you need to STOP doing?

6. After reading this chapter, what do you need to START doing?

7. After reading this chapter, what do you need to CONTINUE doing?

8. What was your biggest takeaway from the chapter?

9. Who would you recommend read this chapter? Be specific.

10. Will you apply what you have learned? Why or why not? How?

Notes Lesson 6 – Unleashing Your Inner Champion

_____

_____

_____

_____

_____

_____

_____

_____

_____

_____

_____

_____

_____

_____

_____

_____

_____

_____

_____

_____

_____

Lesson 7 – F'd UP and Ballin

Curriculum Designed for Educators, Trainers, Students

Lesson 7 – F'd UP and Ballin

Tips for Use

Curriculum may be used as a tool for professional coaching, peer-to-peer coaching, guidance counseling, and career counseling.

Overview

The F'd UP and Ballin lesson introduces participants to playing full out, giving 100 percent effort and 100 percent attitude. Participants discuss the three-point play of leadership and the importance of work ethic, drive, and skill development. The full-court pressure analogy described within the book discusses pressures and how to overcome them. Video links are provided at the end of each chapter to build on what was read in the book. Use links as needed.

Objective

Targeting young adults and emerging leaders, the objective is to teach participants how to lead, make better choices, and adopt better habits.

You Will Need
- ✓ A group leader or facilitator
- ✓ Flip chart or white board
- ✓ Copies of the book, *F'd UP*
- ✓ Notebook or journal
- ✓ Feedback form
- ✓ Markers

Lesson 7 – F'd UP and Ballin

Curriculum Designed for Educators, Trainers, Students

Lesson 7 – F'd UP and Ballin

Before Lesson
Writing Activity: (5-10 min)

1. Ask participants to think of a situation when they did not put forth effort to improve a situation and displayed a negative attitude. For example: a relationship, a group project, a team goal, a shared task, etc.

2. Ask participants to think about what they need to do to improve the situation. Then, take their responses and create an acrostic or poem using the word "BALLIN." For example: I want to improve my relationship with a peer and become a better listener. My acrostic might read: *Be attentive. Ask questions. Listen actively. Lean into the conversation. Incite meaningful dialogue. Never text while talking with someone.*

After Lesson (5-10 min)
1. Ask participants to complete the ten-question feedback form accessible in this book and at www.nolimit2your success.com/forms.
2. Discuss questions as a group. Listen. Ask more questions.
3. Encourage participants to reflect, write, and share.

Small Group Activity - Leadership (20 min)
Break into small groups of four to five. Ask each group to create a new three-point play to leadership. Appoint a scribe. Identify three words that represent leadership. Write responses on flip chart. Make it fun. Use an acronym or an acrostic. Post responses up on the wall.

Large Group Discussion – Better Choices, Better Habits (20 min) Discuss with the group. How do better habits and better choices affect our attitude and effort? What is more important, winning or effort? Why?

Feedback Form

Lesson (circle) 1 2 3 4 5 6 7 8

Respond to the questions honestly after reading the assigned chapter in the book *F'd UP: The UPside of Failure*.

1. Did you find the subject matter in this chapter informative and helpful? Why or why not?

2. What was a new concept or idea you learned in this chapter?

3. How did this chapter help you to deal with failures differently?

4. How did the information in this chapter help change your perspective on failure?

5. After reading this chapter, what do you need to STOP doing?

6. After reading this chapter, what do you need to START doing?

7. After reading this chapter, what do you need to CONTINUE doing?

8. What was your biggest takeaway from the chapter?

9. Who would you recommend read this chapter? Be specific.

10. Will you apply what you have learned? Why or why not? How?

Notes Lesson 7 – F'd UP and Ballin

Lesson 8 – Bad Words. Good Advice.

Curriculum Designed for Educators, Trainers, Young Adults

Lesson 8 – Bad Words. Good Advice.

Tips for Use

Curriculum may be used as a tool for professional coaching, peer-to-peer coaching, guidance counseling, and career counseling.

Overview

The Bad Words Good Advice lesson introduces participants to new definitions and new meanings of common words and how changing the meaning changes the power of the word. Video links are provided at the end of each chapter to build on what was read in the book. Use links as needed.

Objective

Targeting young adults and emerging leaders, the objective is to teach participants how to identify bad words and remove them from their vocabulary. The lesson also teaches how to redefine seemingly bad words and repurpose them in a good way.

You Will Need
- ✓ A group leader or facilitator
- ✓ Flip chart or white board
- ✓ Copies of the book, *F'd UP*
- ✓ Notebook or journal
- ✓ Used, broken, or old objects

Lesson 8 – Bad Words. Good Advice.

Curriculum Designed for Educators, Trainers, Young Adults

Lesson 8 – Bad Words. Good Advice.

Before Lesson

Writing Activity: (5-10 min)

1. Ask participants to pick out an object in the room—preferably an old, used, or broken item. Take the object and create something new with it.
2. Write about the object: *What was its former purpose? What is its new purpose?*

After Lesson (5-10 min)
1. Ask participants to complete the ten-question feedback form accessible in this book and at www.nolimit2your success.com/forms.
2. Discuss questions as a group. Listen. Ask more questions.
3. Encourage participants to reflect, write, and share.

Small Group Activity – Bad Words (20 min)

Break into groups of four to five people. Ask each group to select one to two "bad" words listed in chapter eight. Select words that they use daily. Discuss ways to remove or repurpose those words moving forward. Discuss the steps they need to take to change their vocabulary.

Large Group Discussion (20 min)

As a large group, identify additional "bad" words that are not listed in the book. Get feedback from the group. Which words need to be removed? Which words can be repurposed?

Feedback Form

Lesson (circle) 1 2 3 4 5 6 7 8

Respond to the questions honestly after reading the assigned chapter in the book *F'd UP: The UPside of Failure*.

1. Did you find the subject matter in this chapter informative and helpful? Why or why not?

2. What was a new concept or idea you learned in this chapter?

3. How did this chapter help you to deal with failures differently?

4. How did the information in this chapter help change your perspective on failure?

5. After reading this chapter, what do you need to STOP doing?

6. After reading this chapter, what do you need to START doing?

7. After reading this chapter, what do you need to CONTINUE doing?

8. What was your biggest takeaway from the chapter?

9. Who would you recommend read this chapter? Be specific.

10. Will you apply what you have learned? Why or why not? How?

Notes Lesson 8 – Bad Words. Good Advice.